LETTERS OF NOTE: FATHERS

*Letters of Note* was born in 2009 with the launch of lettersofnote.com, a website celebrating old-fashioned correspondence that has since been visited over 100 million times. The first *Letters of Note* volume was published in October 2013, followed later that year by the first Letters Live, an event at which world-class performers delivered remarkable letters to a live audience.

Since then, these two siblings have grown side by side, with *Letters of Note* becoming an international phenomenon, and Letters Live shows being staged at iconic venues around the world, from London's Royal Albert Hall to the theatre at the Ace Hotel in Los Angeles.

You can find out more at lettersofnote.com and letterslive.com. And now you can also listen to the audio editions of the new series of *Letters of Note*, read by an extraordinary cast drawn from the wealth of talent that regularly takes part in the acclaimed Letters Live shows.

# Letters of Note

# Fathers

COMPILED BY

## Shaun Usher

PENGUIN BOOKS

For Dad

PENGUIN BOOKS
An imprint of Penguin Random House LLC
penguinrandomhouse.com

First published in Great Britain by Canongate Books Ltd 2021
Published in Penguin Books 2021

Pages 157–158 constitute an extension of this copyright page.

Library of Congress Control Number: 2021932101
ISBN 9780143134701 (paperback)
ISBN 9780525506515 (ebook)

Printed in the United States of America
1st Printing

Set in Joanna MT

# CONTENTS

A letter is a time bomb, a message in a bottle, a spell, a cry for help, a story, an expression of concern, a ladle of love, a way to connect through words. This simple and brilliantly democratic art form remains a potent means of communication and, regardless of whatever technological revolution we are in the middle of, the letter lives and, like literature, it always will.

## INTRODUCTION

One cold morning in 2019, as he begrudgingly poked around his mouth with a toothbrush, the youngest of our two sons glanced up at the mirror and, with the confidence and comic timing of someone with much larger teeth, announced, 'Daddy . . . your books are stupid.'

It is with these supportive words in mind that I partially dedicate *Letters of Note: Fathers* to both of my beloved children, without whom this book would likely have arrived more swiftly but from an earlier model of Shaun – an emotionally sturdier version who didn't sense immediate danger in every new environment, wasn't hallucinating from constant sleep deprivation brought on by *six years* of nightly bed intrusions, was failing miserably to fully appreciate and capitalise on the level of freedom he had once enjoyed, and, most importantly, had yet to experience the moment his heart would somehow double in size and sensitivity as he held his bruised firstborn in his arms, priorities instantly shifting to allow space, front and centre, for fatherhood.

The other person to whom I dedicate this

collection of letters is my dad, a magnificent man who brought nothing but warmth and a gentle undercurrent of idiocy to not just my childhood and that of my siblings, but also to that of our delighted friends. A man who often felt more like our taller, hairier brother. A man who, despite working long hours to support his family, never really felt absent. A man whose greatest words of advice to his children, which he repeated so very often but to my eternal frustration never put down in a letter, were, 'Don't talk to strangers unless you know them, and don't answer the phone unless it rings.' Wise words, indeed. It is no exaggeration to say that I hit the jackpot when it came to parents, and my dad will always be the dad that I strive to be. I can only hope that my children feel something even vaguely similar should they ever choose to walk the same path.

It was in April of 2010 that my wife and I walked gingerly out of the maternity ward with our first son. Six months later, filled with a different kind of dread, we carried our six-month-old boy into a different hospital to be faced with what appeared to be the shell of my father, unable to communicate after suffering a stroke that devastated and still affects us all to this day. Those fraught hours, days, weeks and months that followed were the toughest I have experienced, and it is only now, almost a decade later, that I am realising just how worried I was to have almost waved goodbye to him, just as my son, whom I so desperately wanted to experience the joys of knowing my dad, was entering the world. Thankfully, he is still with us in 2019, and my dad's remaining 'good' hand can now be found either kneading dough or loosely clasped around his throat as he's doubled up with laughter – a pose that predates the medical emergency by decades and now serves as proof that the stroke failed to strip him of the most important bits.

*Letters of Note: Fathers* is a collection of thirty letters that explore the relationship between father and child, as complex and varied as such a bond can be. Letters of invaluable paternal advice from the likes of Ted Hughes and Mahatma Gandhi sit amongst angry letters from child to father, including a centuries-old complaint discovered in Egypt, the mood of which feels amusingly modern. A moving exchange between a gay father and his gay son could only have been published in recent years, unlike the correspondence from 2016 in which father and son share their fears around increased police brutality in the US. Elsewhere, an ex-slave writes to his former owner and warns her that he is coming, with assistance, to collect his children. Through it all can be found humour and sadness, hope and fear, pride and frustration. An emotional journey not unlike fatherhood itself.

Shaun Usher
2020

# The Letters

## LETTER 01
## THE MOST GRATEFUL OF PARENTS
Samuel Bernstein to Serge Koussevitzky
*15 September 1941*

*At New York City's Carnegie Hall on 14 November
1943, the life of twenty-five-year-old Leonard
Bernstein changed in an instant when a last-minute
substitution led to him making his conducting debut
with the New York Philharmonic Orchestra. By all
accounts it was a huge success – so much so, in fact,
that the next day he was famous, thus accelerating a
glittering music career that would span decades and
continents and see him held aloft as one of history's
greats. In the summer of 1940, three years before he
was handed that baton, Bernstein had been chosen by
the music director of the Boston Symphony Orchestra,
Serge Koussevitzky, to be one of the conducting
fellows at the Berkshire Music Center in Tanglewood,
an opportunity he grabbed with both hands.
Koussevitzky became Bernstein's idol and mentor, his
love for music intensifying to the point where it was
all he could think about. This development was
noticed by his father, Samuel, who had initially
opposed this obsession of Bernstein's. In September of
1941, acutely aware that his son was destined to
continue on this path, he wrote a letter.*

# THE LETTER

Sept. 15th, 1941

Dr. Serge Koussevitzky
Lenox
Mass.

Dear Sir:
Please forgive this liberty which I am taking in communicating with you but since the matter is an urgent one, I know you will understand my reasons for writing you at this time.

My son, Leonard, has just returned home after a few weeks vacation and, not only from fatherly instinct but from every outward indication, it is quite obvious that Leonard is unhappy for the reason, as you can probably appreciate, that he is so preoccupied with the work upon which he centers his every thought ...... MUSIC. Please forgive this humble parent, therefore, in trespassing upon your privacy but I must, of necessity, appeal to you for some assistance in Leonard's behalf. Quite frankly, Dr. Koussevitzky, Leonard idolizes you; I know what you have come to mean to him and your kind efforts manifested in his behalf is a fair indication of the mutual feeling which exists between you.

It is with great concern that I am now appealing to you to find some opportunity for Leonard so that it will be possible for him to continue with his first Love ...... Music, and in the particular field in which he is so greatly interested. I hope and pray that you may find some opening [for] him somewhere in these United States where he may continue with his work. The financial aspect does not enter into my thoughts for my chief concern is to find some haven for Leonard where he may continue with his work and know happiness.

Please forgive me a thousand times for inflicting my problem upon you but I felt it my duty as Leonard's Father to approach you and knowing you for the type of man you are, I am certain you will understand. May God spare you for many, many years to come so that you may continue with your accomplishments and with the good that you have done in this world and will continue to do and of the many good deeds you have accomplished, one of importance, yes, one I believe very necessary for the future well-being of my Son, will be that which you will accomplish now in his behalf.

I appreciate more than can be expressed by mere

words, your kindness to Leonard and for the interest which you manifested in his interests and you would make this Father, The most grateful of parents, if you would but continue in your efforts. Leonard's pride would never have sanctioned my approach to you in this manner, I know therefore that you will understand my request that this letter be held in strict confidence.

Thank you, Dr. Koussevitzky, and may God bless you!

Respectfully yours,
Samuel J Bernstein

## LETTER 02
## I LOVED THE BOY
William Wordsworth to Robert Southey
*2 December 1812*

*1812 was the darkest of years for William Wordsworth, the English Romantic poet responsible for many enduring masterpieces, including 'I Wandered Lonely as a Cloud' and the posthumously published autobiographical poem The Prelude. In June, his three-year-old daughter, Catherine, died after suffering convulsions; then, on the first day of December, his six-year-old son, Thomas, passed away, having suffered from measles and pneumonia. On 2 December, with both children buried beneath the same tree in the Lake District, William Wordsworth wrote to friend and fellow poet Robert Southey.*

## THE LETTER

December 2, 1812
Wednesday Evening

My dear Friend,
Symptoms of the measles appeared upon my Son
Thomas last Thursday; he was most favorable held
till Tuesday, between ten and eleven at that hour
was particularly lightsome and comfortable; without
any assignable cause a sudden change took place,
an inflammation had commenced on the lungs
which it was impossible to check and the sweet
Innocent yielded up his soul to God before six in
the evening. He did not appear to suffer much in
body, but I fear something in mind as he was of an
age to have thought much upon death a subject to
which his mind was daily led by the grave of his
Sister.

My wife bears the loss of her child with striking
fortitude. For myself dear Southey I dare not say in
what state of mind I am; I loved the boy with the
utmost love of which my soul is capable, and he is
taken from me—yet in the agony of my spirit in
surrendering such a treasure I feel a thousand times
richer than if I had never possessed it. God comfort

and save you and all our friends and us all from a repetition of such trials—O Southey feel for me! If you are not afraid of the complaint, I ought to have said if you have had it come over to us! Best love from everybody—you will impart this sad news to your Wife and Mrs Coleridge and Mrs Lovel and to Miss Barker and Mrs Wilson. Poor woman! She was most good to him—Heaven reward her.

Heaven bless you
Your sincere Friend
W. Wordsworth

## LETTER 03
## GROW UP AS GOOD REVOLUTIONARIES
Che Guevara to his children
*1965–66*

*In 1955, Argentinian-born Che Guevara met Fidel Castro and quickly joined his efforts to oust Fulgencio Batista as leader of Cuba – a revolution in which he would go on to play a major role, and which would lead to Guevara becoming Minister of Industry under Castro's rule. By 1965, Guevara was keen to spread his revolutionary ideas: he began by travelling to what is now the Democratic Republic of the Congo, where he unsuccessfully attempted to train rebel forces in the area, then moved on to Bolivia, where he was ultimately captured by the Bolivian Army and executed on the orders of President René Barrientos. Before he left for Bolivia, he secretly visited his wife back in Cuba and gave her this letter, to be read by his five children in the event of his death.*

## THE LETTER

To my children

Dear Hildita, Aleidita, Camilo, Celia, and Ernesto,

If you ever have to read this letter, it will be because I am no longer with you. You practically will not remember me, and the smaller ones will not remember me at all.

Your father has been a man who acted on his beliefs and has certainly been loyal to his convictions.

Grow up as good revolutionaries. Study hard so that you can master technology, which allows us to master nature. Remember that the revolution is what is important, and each one of us, alone is worth nothing.

Above all, always be capable of feeling deeply any injustice committed against anyone, anywhere in the world. This is the most beautiful quality in a revolutionary.

Until forever, my children. I still hope to see you.

A great big kiss and a big hug from,

Papa

'REMEMBER THAT
REVOLUTION IS WHAT
IS IMPORTANT, AND
EACH ONE OF US,
ALONE IS WORTH
NOTHING'

— *Che Guevara*

## LETTER 04
## OUR DIFFERENCES UNITE US
Sophia Bailey-Klugh and Barack Obama
*2012*

*In an interview in May 2012, Barack Obama became the first sitting US President to publicly endorse same-sex marriage, saying, 'I've just concluded that for me personally it is important for me to go ahead and affirm that I think same-sex couples should be able to get married.' Such a supportive statement was music to the ears of millions, not least Sophia Bailey-Klugh, a ten-year-old girl with two fathers who soon wrote to the President with a request for advice. Much to the delight of her whole family, a reply eventually arrived.*

## THE LETTERS

Dear Barack Obama,

It's Sophia Bailey Klugh. Your friend who invited you to dinner. You don't remember okay that's fine. But I just wanted to tell you that I am so glad you agree that two men can love each other because I have two dads and they love each other. But at school kids think that it's gross and weird but it really hurts my heart and feelings. So I come to you because you are my hero. If you were me and you had two dads that loved each other, and kids at school teased you about it, what would you do?

Please respond!

I just wanted to say you really inspire me, and I hope you win on being the president. You would totally make the world a better place.

Your friend Sophia

P.S. Please tell your daughters Hi for me!

* * *

November 1, 2012
Miss Sophia Bailey-Klugh

Dear Sophia,

Thank you for writing me such a thoughtful letter about your family. Reading it made me proud to be your president and even more hopeful about the future of our nation.

In America, no two families look the same. We celebrate this diversity. And we recognize that whether you have two dads or one mom what matters above all is the love we show one another. You are very fortunate to have two parents who care deeply for you. They are lucky to have such an exceptional daughter in you.

Our differences unite us. You and I are blessed to live in a country where we are born equal no matter what we look like on the outside, where we grow up, or who our parents are. A good rule is to treat others the way you hope they will treat you. Remind your friends at school about this rule if they say something that hurts your feelings.

Thanks again for taking the time to write to me. I'm honored to have your support and inspired by your compassion. I'm sorry I couldn't make it to dinner, but I'll be sure to tell Sasha and Malia you say hello.

Sincerely,
Barack Obama

## LETTER 05
## LIVE LIKE A MIGHTY RIVER
Ted Hughes to Nicholas Hughes
*1986*

*Ted Hughes was arguably one of the greatest English poets. Born in 1930 in Yorkshire, it was in 1957 that he published his first poetry collection,* The Hawk in the Rain, *to critical acclaim. This saw him embark on a career throughout which he was lavished with praise, right up until, and including, the publication of his last and most dramatic collection,* Birthday Letters *– an intimate and powerful account of his relationship with fellow poet Sylvia Plath, who took her own life in 1963. In 1986, twenty-three years after Plath's death, Hughes wrote to their twenty-four-year-old son, Nicholas, and, quite beautifully, advised him to embrace his "childish self" so as to experience life to its fullest. Tragically, during a period of depression in 2009, Nicholas took his own life. He was forty-seven.*

## THE LETTER

Dear Nick,

I hope things are clearing. It did cross my mind,
last summer, that you were under strains of an odd
sort. I expect, like many another, you'll spend your
life oscillating between fierce relationships that
become tunnel traps, and sudden escapes into wide
freedom when the whole world seems to be just
there for the taking. Nobody's solved it. You solve it
as you get older, when you reach the point where
you've tasted so much that you can somehow
sacrifice certain things more easily, and you have a
more tolerant view of things like possessiveness
(your own) and a broader acceptance of the pains
and the losses. I came to America, when I was 27,
and lived there three years as if I were living inside
a damart sock—I lived in there with your mother.
We made hardly any friends, no close ones, and
neither of us ever did anything the other didn't
want wholeheartedly to do. (It meant, Nicholas,
that meeting any female between 17 and 39 was
out. Your mother banished all her old friends, girl
friends, in case one of them set eyes on me—
presumably. And if she saw me talking with a girl
student, I was in court. Foolish of her, and foolish
of me to encourage her to think her laws were

reasonable. But most people are the same. I was quite happy to live like that, for some years.) Since the only thing we both wanted to do was write, our lives disappeared into the blank page. My three years in America disappeared like a Rip Van Winkle snooze. Why didn't I explore America then? I wanted to. I knew it was there. Ten years later we could have done it, because by then we would have learned, maybe, that one person cannot live within another's magic circle, as an enchanted prisoner.

So take this new opportunity to look about and fill your lungs with that fantastic land, while it and you are still there. That was a most curious and interesting remark you made about feeling, occasionally, very childish, in certain situations. Nicholas, don't you know about people this first and most crucial fact: every single one is, and is painfully every moment aware of it, still a child. To get beyond the age of about eight is not permitted to this primate—except in a very special way, which I'll try to explain. When I came to Lake Victoria, it was quite obvious to me that in some of the most important ways you are much more mature than I am. And your self-reliance, your Independence, your general boldness in exposing yourself to new and to-most-people-very-alarming situations, and your phenomenal ability to carry through your plans to the last practical detail (I know it probably doesn't feel like that to you, but that's how it looks to the rest of us, who simply look on in envy), is the sort of real maturity that not one in a thousand ever come near. As you know. But in many other ways obviously you are still childish—how could you not be, you alone among mankind? It's something people don't discuss, because it's something most people are aware of only as a general crisis of sense of inadequacy, or helpless dependence, or pointless loneliness, or a sense of not having a strong enough ego to meet and master inner storms that come from an unexpected angle. But not many people realise that it is, in fact, the suffering of the child inside them. Everybody tries to protect this vulnerable two three four five six seven eight year old inside, and to acquire skills and aptitudes for dealing with the situations that threaten to overwhelm it. So everybody develops a whole armour of secondary self, the artificially constructed being that deals with the outer world, and the crush of circumstances. And when we meet people this is what we usually meet. And if this is the only part of them we meet we're likely to get a rough time, and to end up making 'no contact'. But when you develop a strong divining sense for the child behind that armour, and you make your dealings and negotiations only with

that child, you find that everybody becomes, in a
way, like your own child. It's an intangible thing. But
they too sense when that is what you are appealing
to, and they respond with an impulse of real life,
you get a little flash of the essential person, which is
the child. Usually, that child is a wretchedly isolated
undeveloped little being. It's been protected by the
efficient armour, it's never participated in life, it's
never been exposed to living and to managing the
person's affairs, it's never been given responsibility
for taking the brunt. And it's never properly lived.
That's how it is in almost everybody. And that little
creature is sitting there, behind the armour, peering
through the slits. And in its own self, it is still
unprotected, incapable, inexperienced. Every single
person is vulnerable to unexpected defeat in this
inmost emotional self. At every moment, behind the
most efficient seeming adult exterior, the whole
world of the person's childhood is being carefully
held like a glass of water bulging above the brim.
And in fact, that child is the only real thing in them.
It's their humanity, their real individuality, the one
that can't understand why it was born and that
knows it will have to die, in no matter how crowded
a place, quite on its own. That's the carrier of all the
living qualities. It's the centre of all the possible
magic and revelation. What doesn't come out of that

creature isn't worth having, or it's worth having only as a tool—for that creature to use and turn to account and make meaningful. So there it is. And the sense of itself, in that little being, at its core, is what it always was. But since that artificial secondary self took over the control of life around the age of eight, and relegated the real, vulnerable, supersensitive, suffering self back into its nursery, it has lacked training, this inner prisoner. And so, wherever life takes it by surprise, and suddenly the artificial self of adaptations proves inadequate, and fails to ward off the invasion of raw experience, that inner self is thrown into the front line—unprepared, with all its childhood terrors round its ears. And yet that's the moment it wants. That's where it comes alive—even if only to be overwhelmed and bewildered and hurt. And that's where it calls up its own resources—not artificial aids, picked up outside, but real inner resources, real biological ability to cope, and to turn to account, and to enjoy. That's the paradox: the only time most people feel alive is when they're suffering, when something overwhelms their ordinary, careful armour, and the naked child is flung out onto the world. That's why the things that are worst to undergo are best to remember. But when that child gets buried away under their adaptive and protective shells—he becomes one of the walking dead, a monster. So when you realise you've gone a few weeks and haven't felt that awful struggle of your childish self—struggling to lift itself out of its inadequacy and incompetence—you'll know you've gone some weeks without meeting new challenge, and without growing, and that you've gone some weeks towards losing touch with yourself. The only calibration that counts is how much heart people invest, how much they ignore their fears of being hurt or caught out or humiliated. And the only thing people regret is that they didn't live boldly enough, that they didn't invest enough heart, didn't love enough. Nothing else really counts at all. It was a saying about noble figures in old Irish poems—he would give his hawk to any man that asked for it, yet he loved his hawk better than men nowadays love their bride of tomorrow. He would mourn a dog with more grief than men nowadays mourn their fathers.

And that's how we measure out our real respect for people—by the degree of feeling they can register, the voltage of life they can carry and tolerate—and enjoy. End of sermon. As Buddha says: live like a mighty river. And as the old Greeks said: live as though all your ancestors were living again through you.

## LETTER 06
## YOU ARE YOUR FATHER
Saul Bellow to Martin Amis
*13 March 1996*

*Novelist Martin Amis had a difficult relationship with his
father, Kingsley, a fellow author and poet who was
vocal in his distaste for his son's work. In 1983, Martin
was sent by the* New York Observer *to interview his idol,
Saul Bellow, whom he considered to be the greatest
American writer of all time, and a friendship blossomed.
Twelve years later, after Kingsley suffered a debilitating
stroke and died, Martin reportedly called Bellow and
said, 'You'll have to be my father now,' to which Bellow
is said to have replied, 'Well, I love you very much.' This
letter was written the next year. Bellow makes reference
to his bout of ciguatera fish poisoning in 1994, from
which he nearly died, an experience he fictionalised in
his final novel,* Ravelstein.

## THE LETTER

March 13, 1996
Brookline, Mass.

My dear Martin:

I see that I've become a really bad correspondent.
It's not that I don't think of you. You come into my
thoughts often. But when you do it appears to me
that I owe you a particularly grand letter. And so
you end in the "warehouse of good intentions":

"Can't do it now."

"Then put it on hold."

This is one's strategy for coping with old age,
and with death—because one can't die with so
many obligations in storage. Our clever species, so
fertile and resourceful in denying its weaknesses.

I entered the hospital in '94, a man biologically
in his forties. Coming out in '95, I was the Ancient
Mariner, and the Mariner didn't write novels. He
had only one story and delivered it orally. But
(I told myself) you are a writer still, and perhaps
you'd better come to terms with the Ancient.

I may be about to resolve all these difficulties,
but for two years they have totally absorbed me.

I've become forgetful, too. Nothing like your

father's nominal aphasia. I find I can't remember the names of people I don't care for—in some ways a pleasant disability. I further discover that I would remember people's names because it relieved me from any need to think about them. Their names were enough. Like telling heads.

I can guess how your father must have felt at his typewriter, with a book to finish. My solution is to turn to shorter, finishable things. I have managed to do a few of those. Like learning to walk again—but what if what one wants, really, is to run?

I am sure you have thought these things in watching your father's torments.

Last Saturday I attended a memorial service for Eleanor Clark, the widow of R. P. Warren. I found myself saying to her daughter Rosanna that losing a parent is something like driving through a plate-glass window. You didn't know it was there until it shattered, and then for years to come you're picking up the pieces—down to the last glassy splinter.

Of course you are your father, and he is you. I have often felt this about my own father, whom I half expect to see when I die. But I believe I do know how your father must have felt, sitting at his typewriter with an unfinished novel. Just as I understand your saying that you are your dad. With a fair degree of accuracy I can see this in my own father. He and I never seemed to be in rapport: Our basic assumptions were very different. But that now looks superficial. I treat my sons much as he treated me: out of breath with impatience, and then a long inhalation of affection.

I willingly take up the slack as a sort of adoptive father. I do have paternal feelings towards you. It's not only language that unites us, or "style." We share more remote but also more important premises.

And I'm not actually at the last gasp. I expect to be around for a while (not a prediction but an expectation). "Whilst this machine is to me," Hamlet told Ophelia.

Yours, with love.

## LETTER 07
## DO NOT FORGET YOUR DAD
Richard Harding Davis to Hope Davis
*24 October 1915*

*Richard Harding Davis was a renowned playwright,*
*author and journalist who rose to prominence thanks to*
*his tireless, ground-breaking work as a war correspondent*
*during the Spanish–American War. When he wrote this*
*letter to his daughter, Hope – named after a character in*
*his popular novel* Soldiers of Fortune *– she was nine*
*months old, and he was in France covering the Great*
*War. Six months later, back home in Mount Kisco, New*
*York, after a lengthy deployment overseas, he collapsed*
*and died while dictating a telegram over the phone.*
*Respected and adored by so many, Davis would not be*
*remembered by his daughter, who never had time to*
*know him.*

## THE LETTER

MY DEAR DAUGHTER,

So many weeks have passed since I saw you that by
now you are able to read this without your mother
looking over your shoulder and helping you with
the big words. I have six sets of pictures of you.
Every day I take them down and change them.
Those your dear mother put in glass frames I do
not change. Also, I have all the sweet fruits and
chocolates and red bananas. How good of you to
think of just the things your father likes. Some of
them I gave to a little boy and girl. I play with
them because soon my daughter will be as big.
They have no mother like you, OF COURSE; they
have no mother like YOURS – for except my
mother there never was a mother like yours; so
loving, so tender, so unselfish and thoughtful. If she
is reading this, kiss her for me. These little children
have a little father. He dresses them and bathes
them himself. He is afraid of the cold; and sits in
the sun; and coughs and shivers. His children and I
play hide-and-seek, and, as you will know some
day, for that game there is no such place as a

steamer, with boats and ventilators and masts and alleyways. Some day we will play that game hiding behind the rocks and trees and rose bushes. Every day I watch the sun set, and know that you and your pretty mother are watching it, too. And all day I think of you both.

Be very good. Do not bump yourself. Do not eat matches. Do not play with scissors or cats. Do not forget your dad. Sleep when your mother wishes it. Love us both. Try to know how we love you. THAT you will never learn. Good-night and God keep you, and bless you.

Your Dad

## LETTER 08
## JUST LEAVE ME ALONE!

Anne Frank to Otto Frank

*5 May 1944*

*In 1942, as the Nazis began to occupy the Netherlands, the family of a thirteen-year-old Jewish girl named Anne Frank fled their home and went into hiding in the secret annex of Anne's father's office block in Amsterdam. They were joined, a week later, by another family – the Van Pels – with whom they would co-exist, undetected, for two long years. For the duration of their time there, Anne kept a now-famous diary, which she personified as 'Kitty'. In it she detailed the challenges faced by a teenage girl in such unthinkably difficult circumstances and the strained relationships that existed between Anne and the seven others with whom she was hiding – one of whom, the teenage Peter van Pels, she had begun to fall for. In May of 1944, three months before her family were captured by the Gestapo, Anne wrote to her diary and spoke of a letter to her father.*

## THE LETTER

Dear Kitty,

Father's unhappy with me. After our talk on Sunday
he thought I'd stop going upstairs every evening.
He won't have any of that "Knutscherei" [necking]
going on. I can't stand that word. Talking about it
was bad enough — why does he have to make me
feel bad too! I'll have a word with him today.
Margot gave me some good advice. Here's more or
less what I'd like to say:

> I think you expect an explanation from me,
> Father, so I'll give you one. You're disappointed
> in me, you expected more restraint from me,
> you no doubt want me to act the way a
> fourteen-year-old is supposed to. But that's
> where you're wrong!
>
> Since we've been here, from July 1942
> until a few weeks ago, I haven't had an easy
> time. If only you knew how much I used to
> cry at night, how unhappy and despondent I
> was, how lonely I felt, you'd understand my
> wanting to go upstairs! I've now reached the

point where I don't need the support of Mother or anyone else. It didn't happen overnight. I've struggled long and hard and shed many tears to become as independent as I am now. You can laugh and refuse to believe me, but I don't care. I know I'm an independent person, and I don't feel I need to account to you for my actions. I'm only telling you this because I don't want you to think I'm doing things behind your back. But there's only one person I'm accountable to, and that's me.

When I was having problems, everyone – and that includes you – closed their eyes and ears and didn't help me. On the contrary, all I ever got were admonitions not to be so noisy. I was noisy only to keep myself from being miserable all the time. I was overconfident to keep from having to listen to the voice inside me. I've been putting on an act for the last year and a half, day in, day out. I've never complained or dropped my mask, nothing of the kind, and now . . . now the battle is over. I've won! I'm independent, in both body and mind. I dont need a mother anymore, and I've emerged from the struggle a stronger person.

Now that its over, now that I know the

battle has been won, I want to go my own way, to follow the path that seems right to me. Don't think of me as a fourteen-year-old, since all these troubles have made me older; I won't regret my actions, I'll behave the way I think I should!

Gentle persuasion won't keep me from going upstairs. You'll either have to forbid it, or trust me through thick and thin. Whatever you do, just leave me alone!

Yours, Anne M. Frank

## LETTER 09
## A FATHER IS A MAP OF THE SELF
Rick R. Reed and Nicholas Reed
*2003*

*It wasn't until 2015, thanks to a ruling by the US
Supreme Court in Obergefell v. Hodges, that same-sex
marriage was legalised across the United States. Twelve
years earlier, as Massachusetts became the first US
state to legalise such a partnership, American novelist
Rick R. Reed and his son, both of whom are gay,
exchanged letters on the subject of their sexuality, and
of their hopes for each other in a country that was
slowly beginning to recognise them. Happily, Rick did
eventually dance, and indeed officiate, at his son's
wedding, when Nicholas married his boyfriend, Tarik, on
15 August 2009. Rick followed suit not long afterwards,
marrying his partner in December 2012.*

## THE LETTERS

Dear Son,

When you told me, a couple of years ago, that you were gay, I remember being surprised at my own reaction. I was kind of stunned, and maybe, just a little disappointed. I mean, don't most fathers want their sons to follow in their footsteps? I had imagined you being a writer, like me, although part of me hoped for a less volatile existence. The job description for professional dreamer doesn't always include the things we wish for our children, like security and avoiding the ugly specter of rejection. But I wasn't sure how I felt about you following in my footsteps as a gay man.

I've since grown used to the fact that you are who you are. And now I can look back with a wry smile at my initial reaction. A gay father is the last person one would expect to experience disappointment and shock when his son comes out to him. But I remember one of my first thoughts was, "Well, there go the dreams of dancing at my son's wedding." It's hokey, I know, but that doesn't change the fact that it was one of my initial thoughts.

A thought I did NOT have was, "Well, maybe that will change." It's amazing to me that as little as two summers ago, I didn't hold up much hope for watching you join up with someone special until death do you part. Oh sure, there was the possibility of a civil union, whatever that means. The prospect of dreaming about your kid's civil union just doesn't have the same cachet as imagining a wedding. Nor should it.

And now, here we are, on the brink of another summer, when the newspapers and airwaves are full of talk of gay people getting married. Only last month, gay people started to wed in Massachusetts (even though these weddings, legal as they are, don't hold the same power as a union "between one man and one woman"; one hopes that will change), and I began to think that maybe my disappointment at never seeing my son marry might not have been realistic.

So now I do what I can in the hopes that you will have the option of marrying one day. I speak out to family and friends, and try to convince them that the arguments against gay marriage are, at the root, hateful and discriminatory. I try to help them see that excluding a set of people from publicly declaring their love and commitment and enjoying the same legal rights as anyone else is wrong. I join groups like the Human Rights Campaign and DontAmend.com, all in the hopes that if we fight hard against right-wing bigotry and discriminatory legislation, you might have a different future that I have.

As you know, I tried the "one woman, one man" marriage thing (with your mother, whom I love and always will love) and, because of my orientation, it didn't work, with lots of people getting hurt in the process. While you're beyond the self-denial I went through, I'd like to make sure one thing you don't do like me is make the same mistakes.

Being able to marry the person you love and are sexually attracted to is a very logical hope I have for you. I don't think it's asking too much. You may choose never to get married, or your marriage may fail for different reasons. Or it may be just the sort of union I now have with my partner (whom I cannot marry, but gladly would), full of togetherness, commitment to one another's wellbeing, and the choice we've made to spend the rest of our lives together. My hope for you is that you can find that kind of magic with another person . . . and that your own government recognizes your commitment and love . . . the same government that was, a long, long time ago, put in place to supposedly look out for your welfare, freedom, and happiness.

Of course, I hope that, when people start seeing

that the fabric of civilization is not being ripped apart by gay couples running wild in Massachusetts, they will stop being so threatened. I hope that for myself, so that as I continue to build my future with my partner, we too will have the option of making a public, legal declaration of our commitment. But more, I hope it for you, the person in whose happiness and wellbeing I've always had the greatest investment. My life is probably more than half over; you're just beginning to make the journey. All I can do is continue to hope, to speak out, and to fight for the kind of future I know you're entitled to.

We always want what's best for our children. Your having the choice to marry, I know, is what's best.


Love,
Dad



\* \* \*


Dear Dad,
When you told me you were gay, I couldn't have understood exactly what you meant; I was only five years old. After you had taken the time to explain it to me, the only thing I couldn't understand was

why it was such a big deal to so many people. After all, you were still the same person you were before you had told me with the same qualities — thoughtfulness, compassion, and gentleness — that I had come to respect and admire; and that I still emulate. In light of those virtues, my family's judgments of you as deranged and evil made no sense. Why they thought that pursuing what every human being needs — to love and be loved — was evil, I still don't know. I thought I would crack under the strain of their demands to either hate you or bear the stain of your sin, but I comforted myself with the illusion that this was some peculiar insanity of theirs; that in the wide world outside my grandparents' house everyone was rational and would see you the same way I did. I quickly learned that this was not the case.

In grade school I learned to be ashamed of you, if not inwardly at least outwardly. In a small Catholic school, the child of a single mother is an oddity, and the gossip and rumours about you started almost as quickly amongst parents, teachers, and clergy as it did among my classmates. When the truth found its way into the rumor mill, I learned what the world thought of you, and of me. It was bad enough that my classmates considered you diseased at best, worse that they thought of me as tainted by association, but the real betrayal came when parents, teachers, and clergy back them up. At best they pitied me because of you; at worst they called me degenerate trash, or a mistake. It has been possible to stand up to the assaults from my family, but when a whole community turned on me, I caved. I denied the truth; I told people you had married a woman to try to regain some semblance of legitimacy. I told homophobic jokes, and used "gay" as an insult. It's awfully difficult to grow up ashamed of your origins; for a boy, a father is a map of the self. It only became more difficult as my own homosexuality emerged on a conscious level; my shame deepened.

Years later I have come to terms with all of this; I recognize now that homophobia is irrational, and on some level, insane. But looking back, I have to wonder how much easier it would have been to grow up the son of a gay man if people had valued the romantic love you had to offer instead of reviling you for it. That's why I get so angry now when I hear the champions of family values declaring that we cannot publicly recognize your love for the sake of the children. As a child, the only thing the ban on gay marriage protected me from was the feeling that I was a whole and legitimate person.

In the end though, marriage equality is not about the children. The simple facts that you want to marry, and that your marriage would not harm anyone, are reasons enough to allow it. This is a free country, and we are all better off when we are all truly free. I wish the best to you and your husband, and look forward to the day when everyone will recognize him as such.

Love,
Nick

## LETTER 10
## GROW UP A CHILD OF THE LIGHT
Jawaharlal Nehru to Indira Nehru
*26 October 1930*

*In January 1966, Indira Gandhi became the country's first female prime minister, nineteen years after her father became the first post-independence prime minister of India. Since she was a child, her father had been a lifelong devotee of Mohandas Gandhi and his non-cooperation movement, and she had been raised in the midst of her family's political activity, going on to serve as Nehru's assistant during his tenure. Prior to his premiership, Nehru had served multiple prison terms for his numerous acts of civil disobedience, and in October 1930, shortly before his daughter's thirteenth birthday, he wrote her this letter – the first of 196 he would go on to pen from various prisons in an effort to teach her about the history of the world.*

# THE LETTER

Central Prison, Naini
October 26, 1930

My dear Indira,

On your birthday you have been in the habit of
receiving presents and good wishes. Good wishes
you will have in full measure, but what present can
I send you from Naini prison? My presents cannot
be very material or solid. They can only be of the
air and of the mind and spirit, such goods as a
fairy might have bestowed on you – things that
even the high walls of prison cannot stop.

You know, sweetheart, how I dislike sermonising
and doling out good advice. When I am tempted to
do this, I always think of the story of a "very wise
man" I once read. Perhaps one day you will yourself
read the book which contains this story.

Thirteen hundred years ago, there came a great
traveller from China to India in search of wisdom and
knowledge. His name was Hiuen Tsang, and over the
deserts and mountains of the north he came, braving
many dangers, facing and overcoming many obstacles,
so great was his thirst for knowledge; and he spent
many years in India learning himself and teaching

others, especially at the great University of Nalanda, which existed then near the city that used to be called Pataliputra and is now known as Patna. Hiuen Tsang became very learned himself and he was given the title of "Master of the Law" – the Law of the Buddha – and he journeyed all over India and saw and studied the people that lived in this great country, in those far-off days. Later he wrote a book of his travels and it is this book which contains the story that comes to my mind. It is about a man from South India who came to Karnasuvarna, which was a city somewhere near the modern Bhagalpur, in Bihar; and this man, it is written, wore round his waist copper-plates, and on his head he carried a lighted torch. Staff in hand, with proud bearing and lofty steps, he wandered about in this strange attire. And when anyone asked him the reason for his curious attire, he told him that his wisdom was so great that he was afraid his belly would burst if he did not wear copper-plates round it; and because he was moved with pity for the ignorant people round about him, who lived in darkness, he carried the light on his head.

Well, I am quite sure that there is no danger of my ever bursting with too much wisdom, and so there is no need for me to wear copper-plates. And in any event, I hope that my wisdom, such of it as I possess, does not live in my belly. Wherever it may reside, there is plenty of room still for more of it and there is no chance of there being no room left. If I am so limited in wisdom, how can I pose as a wise man and distribute good advice to others? And so I have always thought that the best way to find out what is right and what is not right, what should be done and what should not be done, is not by giving sermons, but by talking and discussing, and out of discussion sometimes a little bit of truth comes out. I have liked my talks with you and we have discussed many things, but the world is wide and beyond our world lie other wonderful and mysterious worlds; so none of us need ever be bored or imagine, like the very foolish and conceited person whose story Hiuen Tsang has told us, that we have learned everything worth learning and become very wise. And perhaps, it is as well that we do not become very wise; for the very wise, if any such there are, must sometimes feel rather sad that there is nothing more to learn. They must miss the joy of discovery and of learning new things – the great adventure that all of us who care to may have.

I must not, therefore, sermonise. But what am I to do then? A letter can hardly take the place of a talk; at best, it is a one-sided affair. So, if I say anything that sounds like good advice, do not take it as if it were a bad pill to swallow. Imagine that I have made a suggestion to you for you to think over, as if we really were having a talk.

In history we read of great periods in the life of nations, of great men and women, and great deeds performed, and sometimes in our dreams and reveries we imagine ourselves back in those times and doing brave deeds like the heroes and heroines of old. Do you remember how fascinated you were when you first read the story of Jeanne d'Arc, and how your ambition was to be something like her? Ordinary men and women are not usually heroic. They think of their daily bread and butter, of their children, of their household worries and the like. But a time comes when a whole nation becomes full of faith for a great cause, and then even simple, ordinary men and women become heroes, and history becomes stirring and epoch-making. Great leaders have something in them which inspires a whole nation and makes them do great deeds.

The year you were born in – 1917 – was one of the memorable years of history when a great leader, with a heart full of love and sympathy for the poor and suffering, made his people write a noble and never-to-be forgotten chapter of history. In the very month in which you were born, Lenin started the great revolution which has changed the face of Russia and Siberia. And today in India another great leader, also full of love for all who suffer and passionately eager to help them, has inspired our people to great endeavour and noble sacrifice, so that they may again be free and the starving and the poor and the oppressed may have their burdens removed from them. Bapuji lies in prison, but the magic of his message steals into the hearts of India's millions, and men and women, and even little children, come out of their shells and become India's soldiers of freedom. In India today we are making history, and you and I are fortunate to see this happening before our eyes and to take some part ourselves in this great drama.

How shall we bear ourselves in this great movement? What part shall we play in it? I cannot say what part will fall to our lot; but, whatever it may be, let us remember that we can do nothing which may bring discredit to our cause or dishonour to our people. If we are to be India's soldiers, we have India's honour in our keeping, and that honour is a sacred trust. Often we may be in doubt as to what to do. It is no easy matter to decide what is right and what is not. One little test I shall ask you to apply whenever you are in doubt. It may help you. Never do anything in secret or anything that you would wish to hide. For the desire to hide anything means that you are afraid, and fear is a bad thing and unworthy of you. Be brave, and all the rest follows. If you are brave, you will not fear and will not do anything of which you are ashamed. You know that in our great Freedom Movement, under Bapuji's leadership, there is no room for secrecy or hiding. We have nothing to hide. We are not afraid to do what we do and say what we say. We work in the sun and in the light. Even so, in our private lives, let us make friends with the sun and work in the light and do nothing secretly or furtively. Privacy, of course, we may have and should have, but that is a very different thing from secrecy. And if you do so, my dear, you will grow up a child of the light, unafraid and serene and unruffled whatever may happen.

I have written a very long letter to you. And yet there is so much I would like to tell you. How can a letter contain it?

You are fortunate, I have said, in being a witness to this great struggle for freedom that is going on in our country. You are also very fortunate in having a very brave and wonderful little woman for your Mummie, and if you are ever in doubt or in trouble, you cannot have a better friend.

Goodbye, little one, and may you grow up into a brave soldier in India's service!

With all my love and good wishes,

Jawaharlal Nehru

'BE BRAVE, AND ALL THE
REST FOLLOWS'

— *Jawaharlal Nehru*

## LETTER 11
## SO THERE
Theon to Theon
*c*.250 AD

*In 1897, a remarkable letter written on papyrus many centuries ago was discovered in the Egyptian city of Oxyrhynchus, the tone of its content eerily familiar despite its advanced age. Its author was a teenage boy named Theon whose attitude can be accurately described as stroppy. Its recipient, his father, of the same name, would have been amused to know that letters of this flavour would never go out of fashion. The missive is now part of Oxford's Bodleian Library collection.*

## THE LETTER

Theon to his father, Theon, greetings.

A fine thing you did in not taking me to the city with you. If you are not going to take me with you to Alexandria, I won't write you a letter, I won't speak to you, and I won't wish you well. If you go to Alexandria, I won't take your hand or greet you ever again. If you are not going to take me, this is what will happen. My mother told Archelaus that it gets me into a state when I am left out. It was a good thing you sent me some big presents (and some clothes?) on the 12th, the day that you sailed. I'm asking you to send me a lyre. If you don't send one, I won't eat, I won't drink. So there. I pray that you are well.

The 17th of Tubi.
Deliver to Theon from Theon, his son.

## LETTER 12
## YOUR PAPPY
Groucho Marx to Miriam Marx Allen
*26 October 1941*

*Instantly recognisable, thanks to his wildly exaggerated fake moustache and eyebrows, Julius Henry 'Groucho' Marx was one-fifth of the Marx Brothers, a widely lauded comedy act responsible for producing some of the most beloved and funny films of the twentieth century. Unlike most of his siblings, Groucho was popular beyond the family act and continued to work successfully in television long after the brothers called it a day. Groucho had three children, and in 1992 his daughter Miriam published a collection of letters between her and her late father, titled* Love, Groucho, *that went some way to revealing the man behind the moustache. Of those dozens of missives, one of her favourites was this one, written by Groucho in 1941, when Miriam was fourteen.*

# THE LETTER

The Warwick Hotel, New York
October 26, 1941

Dear Darling;

Your mother keeps asking me every day, is there a letter from Miriam?

I keep saying "No" because you wrote in the letter you sent the piece about Grandma, and asked me not to show it to your mother. In the future, if you want to complain about her folks, you will have to write two letters, one to her and one to me.

Well, Kras's show opened and it was a flop. It wasn't bad, but apparently the audiences are sick of plays about Nazis and their problems, and I think it will probably be off the boards in about another week. It's too bad. This is a tough racket, and all the heartaches and sleepless nights make it a pretty thankless profession, unless of course you are one of the lucky few who put over a hit, and then everything looks different, and all the anxious moments are forgotten. Well enough of this philosophizing.

How are you and my dog Duke? You apparently think Duke belongs to you, don't you? Well I had it out with Duke one day when we were together on the bike. I said, Duke, who do you belong to? Miriam or me? He looked up at me and winked. He said, I like Miriam, she is a nice kid and occasionally brushes my coat and throws me a bone, but to compare her to you is sheer folly. Why Groucho old boy, you are my man. That's the first time he had ever called me Groucho, and believe me I was thrilled to my fingertips. He usually calls me Julius, and to hear him saying Groucho affected me deeply. Well anyway, as he trotted along beside the bike he continued, you know I can never forget the hundreds of miles we've done together in rain and sunshine, the dogs I have fought and run from, the cats I have pursued up trees, I've lived my life with you and I can never be any one's but yours.

Well, I miss him a lot and you too. I have never been attached to a dog like I am to this one, no, not even Shep. This is probably because I have been much closer to this one. If you see him around the house, kiss him for me.

I am so glad that Susie is out of danger and that she is on the way to recovery. I like Susie and be sure and give her my best and if you see her around the house, you can kiss her for me along with the dog.

I had a long letter from the Jerk Sisters. They managed to fill up seven or eight pages of trivia with what is going on around Westwood and its environs (in case you are puzzled, environs means neighborhood). My plans are still uncertain, but they are close to the stage where I will certainly make a decision one way or another.

Had a letter from Irv Brecher. He has completed a play and is on the way East with it. I hope he has better luck than Sheekman and Kras had with their plays. It's a tough business this thing of being a playwright and takes a hell of a lot of skill. Kras is a little crushed, but you know Kras; he will bounce right up with something bigger and better. I am glad you are back with George Englund if that's who it is. I think Pascal is a little on the mature side for you, and I would prefer you to go out with boys closer to your age.

Well my queen, I have to go now and do a million things. All my love to you and as many kisses as you will accept.

Your Pappy. Groucho, Julius, Padre, Shorty

## LETTER 13
## ALL WAS OVER
Mary Wollstonecraft Shelley to Mary Hays
*20 April 1836*

*Born in August of 1797, Mary Shelley was just eleven days old when her mother, the noted British proto-feminist and writer Mary Wollstonecraft, died from an infection caught during childbirth. As a result, Shelley was raised by her widowed father, William Godwin, a celebrated novelist and leading political philosopher of the Enlightenment, who was keen for his daughter to also become a writer. His wish came true. In 1818, Shelley's first novel, the enormously influential* Frankenstein, *was published anonymously; three years later, a new edition appeared bearing her name. It remains a classic to this day. In 1836, having been cared for by Shelley in his old age, Godwin died. Shelley described her father's death in this letter, sent two weeks later to Mary Hays, a fellow novelist and feminist who had been friends with both of Shelley's parents.*

# THE LETTER

14 North Bank,
Regents Park,
London

Dear Madam

Having for some months been somewhat of an invalid – the extreme fatigue and anxiety I went through while attending on the last moments of my dearest Father have made me too ill to attend to anything like business. By my Father's will his papers will pass thro' my hands, & your most reasonable request will be complied with. There is nothing more detestable or cruel than the publication of letters meant for one eye only. I have no idea whether any of yours will be found among my Father's papers – any that I find shall be returned to you. – But my health is such that I cannot promise when I can undergo the fatigue of looking over his papers.

You will be glad to hear that one whom you once knew so well, died without much suffering – his illness was a catarrhal fever which his great age did not permit him to combat – he was ill about 10, & confined to his bed 5 days – I sat up several nights with him – & Mrs Godwin was with him when I was not – as he had a horror of being left to servants. His thoughts wandered a good deal but not painfully – he knew himself to be dangerously ill but did not consider his recovery impossible. His last moment was very sudden – Mrs Godwin & I were both present. He was dozing tranquilly, when a slight rattle called us to his side, his heart ceased to beat, & all was over. This happened at a little after 7 on the day of the 7th ins.

My dear Father left it in his will to be placed as near my Mother as possible. Her tomb in St Pancras Church Yd was accordingly opened – at the depth of twelve feet her coffin was found uninjured – the cloth still over it – & the plate tarnished but legible. The funeral was plain and followed only by a few friends – There might have been many more, but being private, we restricted the number. My Son, now sixteen, was among the Mourners.

I have written these few particulars as they cannot fail to interest you. – I am obliged to you for your kind expression of interest – your name is of course familiar to me as one of those women whose talents do honour to our sex – and as the friend of my parents – I have the honor to be, dear madam

Very truly yours
Mary Shelley

## LETTER 14
## MY DEAR SON
John D. Swain to his son
*1908*

*As his son began student life at Yale University in New Haven, Connecticut, in 1908, novelist and screenwriter John Dewell Swain put pen to paper and, as best he could, prepared him for the road ahead; a road he had travelled seventeen years earlier at the same hallowed institution. His long letter of fatherly advice was soon read by others, and then reprinted in the* Yale Alumni Weekly, *proving so popular amongst both students and parents that it appeared again on numerous occasions. By 1922, copies of Swain's letter were apparently being handed to the parents of Yale freshmen in pamphlet form.*

## THE LETTER

MY DEAR SON: I am writing a few things I meant to say to you when we took our last walk together, the day before you left for Yale. I intended to say them then, and I will even confess that I shamelessly inveigled you into taking a stroll on the quiet street that I might rehearse a carefully prepared bit of Chesterfield up-to-date; but somehow I could not seem to begin, — and, after all, perhaps I can write what was in my mind more freely and plainly than I could have spoken it.

I think I had never realized before that I was getting old.

Of course I have known that my hair is causing your mother much solicitude, and that I am hopelessly wedded to my pince-nez while reading my daily paper, and at the opera; but in some incomprehensible way I had forgotten to associate these trifles with the encroachments of time. It was the sudden realization that you were about to become a Freshman in the college from which, as it seems to me, I but yesterday graduated, that "froze the genial current of my soul," and spared you my paternal lecture.

Why, I can shut my eyes and still hear the Ivy Song, as we sang it that beautiful June morning;

and yet but a few nights more and you will be locked in the deadly Rush on the same field where I triumphantly received two blackened eyes, and, I trust, gave many more!

Another thing, trifling in itself, opened my eyes to the fact of my advancing years.

My son, my loyal and affectionate boy, some day it may be yours to know the pain, the unreasonable pain that comes over a man to know that between him and his boy, and his boy's friends, an unseen but unassailable barrier has arisen, erected by no human agency; and to feel that while they may experience a vague respect and even curiosity to know what exists on your side of the barrier, you on your part would give all, — wealth, position, influence, honor, to get back to theirs! All the world, clumsily or gracefully, is crawling over this barrier; but not one ever crawls back again!

You have ever seemed happy to be with me; you have worked with me, read and smoked with me, even played golf with me; but the subtle change in your attitude, the kindling of your eye when we met young men of your age, is the keenest pain I have ever known; yet one which, God knows! I would not reproach you with.

It explains what I used to see on my father's face and did not understand.

For the tyranny of youth, my son, is the one tyranny which never has been, never can be overthrown. Nothing can displace it, nothing shake its power.

I usually beat you at golf, and occasionally at tennis; I suppose that if we were to spar together I might still make a respectable showing, and at least "save my face." It avails nothing. I am on my side of the barrier, you on yours.

It seems but a year and a day since I tucked the ball under my arm and sped down the gridiron, sustained by the yells of my partisans; and if our game lacked the machine-like precision of the mass formations you are already somewhat familiar with, it was a good game, and we were good men, and all on the right side of the barrier!

So bear with me if I pause a moment and gaze back across this inevitable gulf into the pleasant land that lies behind me, — a picture evoked by your dawning college career.

I would not have you think me regretful, or melancholy. Life has been good to me — and every age has its gifts for the man who is willing to work for them and use them temperately. And nothing is more ungraceful, more ludicrous, than the spectacle of one who attempts to linger over the pleasures of an age he had outlived, and ignore the advantages of his own time of life.

Yet, as the years bring weakness, the mind persistently drifts back to the earlier periods of life, until the aged actually enter a phase we not inaptly name "second childhood," from which Heaven forefend me!

I can still appreciate a pair of sparkling blue eyes, and I am not oblivious to the turn of a pretty shoulder; although I devoutly trust that my interest is now impersonal, and merely artistic . . .

Some fathers say to their sons upon the first home leaving, — "Beware of wine and women!" I do not.

If your home life has not taught you the virtues of a temperate, clean life, as I hope, then no words of mine can do it, and you must learn, as too many others have, from a bitter intimacy with its antithesis.

As to women, I never avoided them; I sought them out, from the time when, a red-cheeked youngster, I trudged to school beside a red-cheeked lassie — asleep these many years in the little village lot where lie so many with whom I fought and played these many years gone by.

I have no advice to offer you on this great subject; its ethics are not taught by letter. If I have any regrets, they are not for your ear, nor any man's. And if, of some women I have known, I cannot say that I lifted them up, at least of no woman can it be said that I thrust her down!

I ask of you no more than this and the guidance

of your own heart; that, in the latter years, when you, too, pass over the barrier, you may not leave behind you shadows on the flower-decked meadows of your youth.

You will probably play cards in college; most men do, — I did. The gambling instinct in man is primordial. Kept under due bounds, if not useful, it is at least comparatively harmless. This is the very best that I or any honest man can say of it. I should be glad if you never cared to gamble; but I do not ask it. Assuming that you will, I do not insult you, and myself equally, by warning you against unfairness; to suppose you capable of cheating at cards is to suppose an impossibility. You could not do so without forfeiting the right ever to enter your home again. But some careless and insidious practices, not unknown in my day and class, savor to the upright mind of cheating, without always incurring its penalties.

To play with men whom you know cannot afford to lose, and who must either cheat or suffer privation; to play when you yourself must win your bet to square yourself; that is, when you do not reasonably see how you are going to raise the money to pay providing you lose, — this is a gambler's chance to which no gentleman will ever expose his fellow players.

There is nothing heroic about these desperate casts of the die; one risks only the other fellow's money. These practices I ask and expect you to avoid.

I ask nothing of you in the way of a declared position on religion. Your mother may have demanded more of you here, — entreated more; I cannot. I ask but this: that you will give earnest, serious consideration to the fact that we exist on this planet for a shockingly brief fraction of Eternity; that it behooves every man to diligently seek an answer to the great question, — Why am I here? And then, as best he can, to live up to the ideal enjoined by his answer. And if this carries you far, and if it leads you to embrace any of the great creeds of Christendom, this will be to your mother an unspeakable joy, and perhaps not less so to me; but it is a question which cannot be settled by the mere filial desire to please.

Last of all, while you are in college, be of it and support its every healthful activity.

I ask no academic honor your natural inclinations may not lead you to strive for; no physical supremacy your animal spirits may not instinctively reach out and grasp.

You will, I presume, make the fraternity I made, and, I hope, the societies; you will probably then learn that your father was not always a dignified, bearded man in pince-nez and frock coat, and that on his side of the barrier he cut not a few capers which, seen in the clear light of his summer, gain little grace. Yet, were he to live his life over again, he would cut the same, or worse.

Finally, if you make any of the teams, never quit. That is all the secret of success. Never quit!

Quitting, I like to believe, has not been a striking characteristic of our family, and it is not tolerated in our college.

If you can't win the scholarship, fight it out to the end of the examination.

If you can't win your race, at least finish — somewhere.

If your boat can't win, at least keep pulling on your oar, even if your eye glazes and the taste of blood comes into your throat with every heave.

If you cannot make your five yards in football, keep bucking the line — never let up — if you can't see, or hear, keep plugging ahead! Never quit! If you forget all else I have said, remember these two words, through all your life, and come success or failure, I shall proudly think of you as my own dear son.

And so, from the old home-life, farewell, and Godspeed!

Your Affectionate Father

'. . . NEVER QUIT. THAT
IS THE SECRET OF
SUCCESS. NEVER QUIT!'

— John D. Swain

## LETTER 15
## SHE IS BALD
Arthur Conan Doyle to his mother
*28 January 1889*

*One morning in January of 1889, Sherlock Holmes
creator Arthur Conan Doyle wrote to his mother with
the news that he had become a father for the first
time with the birth of his daughter, Mary Louise.
A son, Kingsley, followed three years later, by which
time he had given up his struggling medical practice to
focus on his literary career. Their mother, Louise
('Toodles'), died of tuberculosis in 1906, and soon
afterward Conan Doyle married Jean Leckie. Conan
Doyle and Jean had three more children together, and
upon his death he bequeathed to them all the royalties
from his many published works. Kingsley died at the
age of twenty-six during the influenza pandemic of
1918. Mary died alone, an impoverished spinster, at
eighty-seven.*

## THE LETTER

Jan 28 1889

Southsea

Toodles produced this morning at 6.15 a
remarkably fine specimen of the Toodles minor,
who is now howling her head off in the back
bedroom. I must say that I am surprised at the
conduct of the young woman, seeing that both her
parents are modest sort of people. She came
evidently for a long visit, and yet she has made no
apology for the suddenness of her arrival. She had
no luggage with her, nor any possessions of any
kind, barring a slight cough, and a voice like a
coalman. I regret to say that she had not even any
clothes, and we have had for decency's sake to rig
her out with a wardrobe. Now one would not
mind doing all this for the sake of a visitor, but
when the said visitor does nothing but snuffle in
reply it becomes monotonous. She has frank and
engaging manners, but she is bald, which will
prevent her from going out into society for some
little time.

Forgive me for not telling you, dear. I knew how trying the suspense of waiting would be, and thought that on the whole it would be best that you should learn when it was too late to worry yourself.

P. S. Tell Lottie her flannel square came in very useful for the young Empress—her first bit of property

## LETTER 16
## WE ALL MAKE MISTAKES
Sheriff Anwar to Julie and Brian
*March 2017*

*In March 2017, at the end of a particularly bitter custody case that resulted in the father being granted indirect contact with his three children, a clinical psychologist advised the presiding judge, Sheriff Aisha Anwar, to break from tradition and delicately communicate the Scottish court's decision to those children by letter. The psychologist then read the letter to its recipients. With the names of all parties anonymised, Sheriff Anwar's missive was then published by the court to wide acclaim.*

## THE LETTER

Dear Julie and Brian

My name is Sheriff Anwar.

Your mum and dad have asked me to make a decision on whether you should see your dad.

I think that as my decision is all about you, it is only fair that I should write to you.

I have not met you, but I have heard a lot about you. You mum has told me all about how you are getting on at school and about your likes and dislikes. Your dad has told me about all the things you used to do together.

Your mum and dad have also told me about the problems they have had with each other after they split up. Sometimes, when parents split up it is very hard for them to stay friends. Your mum and dad have found it very hard to stay friends. Sometimes when people are no longer friends, they can say some nasty things about each other. They forget what is good about each other. That is not right and it is not nice. It shouldn't happen. You should not have to hear any of that. That is for the adults to sort out.

I have listened carefully to what everyone has said. It's my job to listen carefully and then decide what is best for you.

Your mum, dad, and other members of your family have all spoken to me. I have also listened to what Dr Khan has said. I know, from what your mum and Dr Khan have told me, that you don't want to see your dad.

I can understand that. Your dad's job is to care for you, protect you, love you, help you, make good plans for you and to know what is right for you. Sometimes, he has not been very good at that. He has locked you in your rooms when you have been naughty and you haven't liked that. He has sworn at you sometimes and you haven't liked that. When you were younger, he washed you and he was a bit rough, and you didn't like that. He asked Mrs McCormick to move into his house and he took her on holiday with you, without telling you first. He should not have done that. That was not fair of him. He should have talked to you first so that you knew what was happening and why.

But I don't believe that your dad meant to hurt you or to be mean to you in doing the things that he has done. I believe that he did not really think about how you would feel. That does not make him a bad dad. I know that there are lots of things that you did together that you really enjoyed, like playing in the garden, skiing and going on holidays. I know that he used to help you with homework,

make your dinner and pick you up from school. I
know that he has kept in touch with the school to
learn about your progress.

There is a good side to your dad. He really wants
to make things better with you. He wants to be your
dad. He wants to love and care for you. He wants to
spend time with you. He has told me that he will
do anything he has to do to make things right.

I think that your dad needs some help to
understand how you are feeling and to understand
how he can be a better dad to you. I think that your
dad needs some help to make sure he doesn't make
the same mistakes. I have asked him to get that help
and he has agreed. He might also, sometimes, need
some help from you to understand how you feel.

I think your mum also needs some help to be
better able to support you and to be more positive
about your dad. She has agreed. I hope that she
will now focus on helping you to see the good in
your dad. She has told me that she will support
you in getting to know your dad again, if that is
what I decide is the right thing for you.

I have also asked your mum and dad to get
some help so that they can talk to each other again,
even if they can't be good friends.

So, I have thought about all of this very carefully.
I have especially thought about how you feel.

I don't think that it is good for you to grow up thinking you have a bad dad. I don't think that it is good for you to forget all the good times. I don't think that is it good for you to think that your dad meant to hurt you, when he didn't. I think that it is better for you to get to know your dad again and to give him a chance to make things better.

I have asked Dr Khan to meet with you and to help you to understand my decision. I have decided that your dad should write to you once a month, so that you can start to get to know each other again. I hope that you will feel able to write back to him.

We all make mistakes. The important thing is that we learn from them. I think your dad has learned from his mistakes.

I hope that my letter explains to you why I have made this decision.

Sheriff Anwar

## LETTER 17
## THINKING SO MUCH AND SO OFTEN
## OF YOU
Nicola Sacco to Dante Sacco
*17 August 1927*

*On 14 July 1921, Ferdinando Nicola Sacco and fellow*
*Italian immigrant and anarchist Bartolomeo Vanzetti*
*were convicted of murdering two men during an armed*
*robbery in Braintree, Massachusetts. Whether or not*
*they were actually guilty has never been determined,*
*but they professed their innocence to the end. When*
*Sacco was arrested, his son, Dante, was seven, and on*
*his visits to his father they played together by*
*throwing a ball back and forth over the prison wall.*
*Years of appeals and hunger strikes could not save*
*Sacco, and one week after he penned this letter he and*
*Vanzetti were executed. Fifty years later, Massachusetts*
*Governor Michael S. Dukakis concluded the men did*
*not receive a fair trial and declared 23 August to be*
*Nicola Sacco and Bartolomeo Vanzetti Memorial Day.*

# THE LETTER

August 18, 1927.

MY DEAR SON AND COMPANION:

Since the day I saw you last I had always the idea
to write you this letter, but the length of my
hunger strike and the thought I might not be able
to explain myself, made me put it off all this time.

The other day, I ended my hunger strike and just
as soon as I did that I thought of you to write to
you, but I find that I did not have enough strength
and I cannot finish it at one time. However, I want
to get it down in any way before they take us again
to the death-house, because it is my conviction that
just as soon as the court refuses a new trial to us
they will take us there. And between Friday and
Monday, if nothing happens, they will electrocute
us right after midnight, on August 22nd. Therefore,
here I am, right with you with love and with open
heart as ever I was yesterday.

I never thought that our inseparable life could
be separated, but the thought of seven dolorous
years makes it seem it did come, but then it has
not changed really the unrest and the heart-beat of

affection. That has remained as it was. More. I say
that our ineffable affection reciprocal, is today more
than any other time, of course. That is not only a
great deal but it is grand because you can see the
real brotherly love, not only in joy but also and
more in the struggle of suffering. Remember this,
Dante. We have demonstrated this, and modesty
apart, we are proud of it.

Much we have suffered during this long Calvary.
We protest today as we protested yesterday. We
protest always for our freedom.

If I stopped hunger strike the other day, it was
because there was no more sign of life in me.
Because I protested with my hunger strike yesterday
as today I protest for life and not for death.

I sacrificed because I wanted to come back to
the embrace of your dear little sister Ines and your
mother and all the beloved friends and comrades of
life and not death. So Son, today life begins to
revive slow and calm, but yet without horizon and
always with sadness and visions of death.

Well, my dear boy, after your mother had talked
to me so much and I had dreamed of you day and
night, how joyful it was to see you at last. To have
talked with you like we used to in the days — in
those days. Much I told you on that vist and more
I wanted to say, but I saw that you will remain the

same affectionate boy, faithful to your mother who loves you so much, and I did not want to hurt your sensibilities any longer, because I am sure that you will continue to be the same boy and remember what I have told you. I knew that and what here I am going to tell you will touch your sensibilities, but don't cry Dante, because many tears have been wasted, as your mother's have been wasted for seven years, and never did any good. So, Son, instead of crying, be strong, so as to be able to comfort your mother, and when you want to distract your mother from the discouraging soulness, I will tell you what I used to do. To take her for a long walk in the quiet country, gathering wild flowers her and there, resting under the shade of trees, between the harmony of the vivid stream and the gentle tranquility of the mothernature, and I am sure that she will enjoy this very much, as you surely would be happy for it. But remember always, Dante, in the play of happiness, don't you use all for yourself only, but down yourself just one step, at your side and help the weak ones that cry for help, help the prosecuted and the victim, because that are your better friends; they are the comrades that fight and fall as your father and Bartolo fought and fell yesterday for the conquest of the joy of freedom for all and the poor workers.

In this struggle of life you will find more love and you will be loved.

I am sure that from what your mother told me about what you said during these last terrible days when I was lying in the iniquitous death-house — that description gave me happiness because it showed you will be the beloved boy I had always dreamed.

Therefore, whatever should happen tomorrow, nobody knows, but if they should kill us, you must not forget to look at your friends and comrades with the smiling gave of gratitude as you look at your beloved ones, because they love you as they love every one of the fallen persecuted comrades. I tell you, your father that is all the life to you, your father that loved you and saw them, and knows their noble faith (that is mine) their supreme sacrifice that they are still doing for our freedom, for I have fought with them, and they are the ones that still hold the last of our hope that today they can still save us from electrocution, it is the struggle and fight between the rich and the poor for safety and freedom, Son, which you will understand in the future of your years to come, of this unrest and struggle of life's death.

Much I thought of you when I was lying in the death house — the singing, the kind tender voices of the children from the playground, where there was all the life and the joy of liberty – just one step from the wall which contains the buried agony of three buried souls. It would remind me so often of you and your sister Ines, and I wish I could see you every moment. But I feel better that you did not come to the death-house so that you could not see the horrible picture of three lying in agony waiting to be electrocuted, because I do not know what effect it would have on your young age. But then, in another way if you were not so sensitive it would be very useful to you tomorrow when you could use this horrible memory to hold up to the world the shame of the country in this cruel persecution and unjust death. Yes, Dante, they can crucify our bodies today as they are doing, but they cannot destroy our ideas, that will remain for the youth of the future to come.

Dante, when I said three human lives buried, I meant to say that with us there is another young man by the name of Celestino Maderios that is to be electrocuted at the same time with us. He has been twice before in that horrible death-house, that should be destroyed with the hammers of real progress – that horrible house that will shame forever the future of the citizens of Massachusetts. They should destroy that house and put up a factory or school, to teach many of the hundreds of the poor orphan boys of the world.

Dante, I say once more to love and be nearest to your mother and the beloved ones in these sad days, and I am sure that with your brave heart and kind goodness they will feel less discomfort. And you will also not forget to love me a little for I do — O, Sonny! thinking so much and so often of you.

Best fraternal greetings to all the beloved ones, love and kisses to your little Ines and mother. Most hearty affectionate embrace.

Your father and companion

P.S. Bartolo send you the most affectionate greetings. I hope that your mother will help you to understand this letter because I could have written much better and more simple, if I was feeling good. But I am so weak.

## LETTER 18
## IT COULD GO TWO WAYS WITH US
Kurt Vonnegut to Nanette Vonnegut
*13 November 1971*

*In 1947, Kurt Vonnegut became a father for the first time when his wife, Jane, gave birth to their son, Mark. Two years later, a daughter, Edith, arrived, followed by another girl, Nanette, in 1954. Four years later, tragedy struck when Vonnegut's sister, Alice, and her husband, James, both died in the space of forty-eight hours, resulting in their three orphaned sons being swiftly adopted by the Vonneguts. In 1969, as his opus Slaughterhouse-Five was published to wide acclaim, Vonnegut's family life began to crumble, and in 1971 he separated from Jane and moved to Manhattan. It was from there, in November of that year, that he wrote these letters to his youngest daughter.*

# THE LETTERS

Dear old Nan—
Well—it could go two ways with us: you could
figure you had been ditched by your father, and
you could mourn about that. Or we could keep in
touch and come to love each other even more than
we have before.

The second possibility is the attractive one for me.
It's the absolutely necessary one for me. And the
trouble with it is that you will have to write me a
lot, or some, anyway, and call up sometimes, and so
on. We've got to wish each other happy birthdays,
and ask how work is going, and tell each other jokes,
and all that. And you've got to visit me often, and
I've got to pay more attention to what sorts of things
are really good times instead of chores for you.

Jane and I get along very well these days. Our
letters to each other are friendly—and the telephone
calls, too. We feel friendlier and more open with each
other than we have for years: no more fighting while
wearing masks. Things would have gotten much
worse if we had kept going the way we were going—
and life would have looked much uglier to you.

Your mother and father like each other a lot, something you must have doubted sometimes in the past. And we both want you to go to Austria next semester. The drawback to that trip is that you will be expected to write us a lot of letters. But do it anyway. If I were younger, I think I might try to become a European. It's friendlier and cheaper and tastier over there, but you will make at least one really unpleasant discovery: they are wrecking their air and water, too. The Mediterranean is turning into an open sewer, too, just like Lake Erie. I hope that during your lifetime it will be cleaned up again.

I love you as much as I love anybody in the world.
K

* * *

November 20, 1971
New York City

Dear Old Nanno—

That was a keen letter—and you don't have to write too many of those. It's just nice to know that there will be more than just black velvet silence out there, that a pleasant and interesting letter will drift in from time to time.

You're learning now that you do not inhabit a solid, reliable social structure—that the older you get people around you are worried, moody, goofy human beings who themselves were little kids only a few days ago. So home can fall apart and schools can fall apart, usually for childish reasons—and what have you got? A space wanderer named Nan.

And that's O.K. I'm a space wanderer named Kurt, and Jane's a space wanderer named Jane, and so on. When things go well for days on end, it is an hilarious accident.

You are dismayed at having lost a year, maybe, because the school fell apart. Well—I feel as though I've lost the years since Slaughterhouse-Five was published, but that's malarky. Those years weren't lost. They simply weren't the way I'd planned them. Neither was the year in which Jim had to stay motionless in bed while he got over TB. Neither was the year in which Mark went crazy, then put himself together again. Those years were adventures. Planned years are not.

I look back on my own life, and I wouldn't change anything, not even the times when I was raging drunk. I don't drink much any more, by the way. And a screwy thing is happening, without any encouragement from anywhere—I am eating less and less meat.

Other ideas which seem good to me appear uninvited—when I'm alone, and I'm alone a lot. I love being alone sometimes. And one of those ideas is that you are a European, were probably born one. Europe, maybe Austria, is in your DNA. I see you going to the art school where young Ted Rowley is now this coming summer. You will become fluent in German and then French. And maybe you'll get me over there. Maybe that's where I belong, too. We'd live in separate houses, of course. Probably separate countries, even. I wouldn't barge in on you and stay.

I think it's important to live in a nice country rather than a powerful one. Power makes everybody crazy.

Learn German during your last semester at Sea Pines, and you'll learn more than I ever learned in high school. I doubt that they can get you in shape to cool the college boards, so the hell with the college boards. Educate yourself instead. In the final analysis, that's what I had to do, what Uncle Beaver had to do, what we all have to do.

I am going to order you to do something new, if you haven't done it already. Get a collection of the short stories of Chekhov and read every one.

Then read "Youth" by Joseph Conrad. I'm not suggesting that you do these things. I am ordering you to do them.

Any time you want to come here, do it. I have no schedule to upset, no secrets to hide, no privacy to guard from you.

Love— K

# THE STRUGGLE MUST CONTINUE, FOR OUR FUTURE'S SAKE

Eddie Glaude and Langston Glaude
*2016*

*In the early hours of 5 July 2016, a thirty-seven-
year-old black man named Alton Sterling was fatally
shot at close range whilst pinned down by two white
police officers in Baton Rouge, Louisiana. This was
merely the latest in a succession of deaths to have
provoked nationwide protests and intensified debate
about the mistreatment of African-Americans at the
hands of law enforcement officers – a systemic
problem, which in 2013 resulted in the formation of the
Black Lives Matter movement. Shortly after Sterling
was killed, Princeton professor Eddie Glaude and his
son, Langston, exchanged letters in which they
reflected on this crisis and their continued dedication
to the fight for social justice.*

## THE LETTERS

Dear Langston,

I thought of you when I saw the son of Alton
Sterling weeping at a press conference. It was the
latest of a string of haunting public rituals of grief.
The police had killed another black person. His
cries made me think of you. It seems, ever since
the murder of Trayvon Martin—and you were only
fifteen then—that you have had to come to terms
with this pressing fact: that police can wantonly kill
us, and there seems to be little or no protection.
That even I can't protect you.

I remembered that day when the grand jury in
Cleveland declined to indict the police officers who
killed Tamir Rice. We were in an airport, traveling
home. You cursed out loud and paced liked a
trapped animal. I didn't know how to speak to
your rage. It was familiar to me, but I didn't know
what to say. How could I keep it from seeping in
and coloring your soul a deep shade of blue? And
when I read your Facebook posts in response to the
death of Sterling and Philando Castile, I felt the
sting of your anger. It too was familiar. You are
your grandfather's and father's child.

James Baldwin wrote—and you know how
much I love Baldwin—in "The Uses of the Blues"

that "in every generation, ever since Negroes have been here, every Negro mother and father has had to face that child and try to create in that child some way of surviving this particular world, some way to make the child who will be despised not despise himself." He wrote that in 1964, and here we are in 2016, and I am worried about the state of your spirit—worried that the ugliness of this world and the nastiness of some of the white people who inhabit it might dirty you on the inside. Might take away your infectious smile and replace it with a permanent scowl.

I find myself more often than not, and upon reflection this is an astonishing thing to say no less think, wishing you were seven years old again. You were adorable at seven. The vexations of the teenage years were far off, and you still liked me. But I say this not because I find having an empty nest unbearable, although at times I do, or that I long to raise a teenager again—and eventually you would be that maddening teenager again. I just say it because I feel that you would be safer at home, with us.

Those tears, son, shook me. Diamond Reynolds's four-year-old baby consoling her mother made me tremble. I love you, and I don't know what I would do if anything ever happened to you. But I am proud to see your radical rage—your refusal to believe what this world says about you. Keep fighting. And remember, as your grandmother reminds me with all of the wisdom that Mississippi living can muster, that I won't stop worrying about you until I die.

Love,
Dad


* * *


Dear Dad,
When I saw those videos of Alton Sterling and Philando Castile, I thought of you and mom. I thought of Michael Brown's mother and the emotions she felt when they stole her son from her, and I wondered about the pain and anguish you both would feel if that was me in those videos. Then I, too, saw the video of Alton Sterling's son, and I thought about if it had been one of you in those videos, stolen from me by a trigger-happy policeman. The thought alone triggered emotions inside me that I didn't know existed. I wept.

I remember when I first really started getting into activism. You were always checking up on me, making sure I was safe and that I was being careful about what I said and who I said it to. I thought you were being your typical dad self, over-protective of your little boy. I also remember when I started getting death threats on Facebook and Twitter. A neo-Nazi group had put my picture up on their Twitter page. I was terrified. I ran to you.

You may not have known it then, but your presence at the time was perhaps one of the most important things that could have happened to me. On the outside I appeared to be able to keep my composure, but on the inside I was scared. With a single tweet, my confidence and feeling of safety was shattered. To be honest, I almost didn't want to go outside. The world seemed like it was doing everything in its power to destroy me. I was overwhelmed. And despite your parental instincts, which I know were screaming to pull me off social media, you pushed me to reach higher, to stand by the right, and to rise above the ugliness I was experiencing. You taught me that fear is natural, but it's what we do in the face of fear that determines what kind of person we want to be. I will never forget those words. They motivated me. It was exactly what I needed to hear.

In these times of injustice, great anger and grief, I find myself consistently asking, "What would my father do?" Crazy, right? I'm actually listening to your advice for once. But it's your advice that keeps me going. It's what you taught me that keeps me pushing for justice. It's knowing that you love and support me that gives me some sense of safety in this cruel world. And that is everything I need.

Funny, I too find myself wishing that I were a kid again. The world seemed so much simpler back then. But then I remember Tamir Rice. I remember Trayvon Martin, Michael Brown and Aiyana Jones. I look at the faces of countless black bodies piling up in our streets. And I remember my own experiences with police officers as a kid. The struggle must continue, for our future's sake.

I love you, Dad.

Langston

'I AM PROUD TO SEE
YOUR RADICAL RAGE —
YOUR REFUSAL TO
BELIEVE WHAT THIS
WORLD SAYS ABOUT
YOU'

— *Eddie Glaude*

## LETTER 20
## BROWN IS AS PRETTY AS WHITE
W.E.B. Du Bois to Yolande Du Bois
*29 October 1914*

*W.E.B. Du Bois accomplished more than most during a lifetime rich with admirable achievements. In 1895, he became the first African-American to earn a PhD at Harvard; he co-founded, in 1909, the National Association for the Advancement of Colored People, an organisation that has fought tirelessly for racial equality since its inception; and his influential 1903 book on race, The Souls of Black Folk, is considered a classic in its field. Such was his contribution to society that in 1976 the land on which his family home once stood was recognised by the US government as a National Historic Landmark.*

*In 1914, his soon-to-be fourteen-year-old daughter, Yolande, left the family home to study at Bedales School in England. Soon after she arrived, he wrote to her with some words of advice.*

# THE LETTER

New York, October 29, 1914

Dear Little Daughter:

I have waited for you to get well settled before
writing. By this time I hope some of the strangeness
has worn off and that my little girl is working hard
and regularly.

Of course, everything is new and unusual. You
miss the newness and smartness of America.
Gradually, however, you are going to sense the
beauty of the old world: its calm and eternity and
you will grow to love it.

Above all remember, dear, that you have a great
opportunity. You are in one of the world's best
schools, in one of the world's greatest modern
empires. Millions of boys and girls all over this
world would give almost anything they possess to
be where you are. You are there by no desert or
merit of yours, but only by lucky chance.

Deserve it, then. Study, do your work. Be honest,
frank and fearless and get some grasp of the real
values of life. You will meet, of course, curious
little annoyances. People will wonder at your dear
brown and the sweet crinkley hair. But that simply

is of no importance and will soon be forgotten. Remember that most folk laugh at anything unusual, whether it is beautiful, fine or not. You, however, must not laugh at yourself. You must know that brown is as pretty as white or prettier and crinkley hair as straight even though it is harder to comb. The main thing is the YOU beneath the clothes and skin—the ability to do, the will to conquer, the determination to understand and know this great, wonderful, curious world. Don't shrink from new experiences and custom. Take the cold bath bravely. Enter into the spirit of your big bed-room. Enjoy what is and not pine for what is not. Read some good, heavy, serious books just for discipline: Take yourself in hand and master yourself. Make yourself do unpleasant things, so as to gain the upper hand of your soul.

Above all remember: your father loves you and believes in you and expects you to be a wonderful woman.

I shall write each week and expect a weekly letter from you.

Lovingly yours,

Papa

## LETTER 21
## YOU'LL *LOVE* OUR LITTLE CLUB
Dashiell Hammett to Josephine Hammett
*24 May 1944*

*In the mid-1920s, shortly after the birth of their second daughter, Josephine Hammett was informed by medical professionals that her husband, celebrated detective novelist Dashiell Hammett, should no longer live with the family as his relapsing tuberculosis posed a danger to them – in particular, to their children. From that point on, they lived apart, with Hammett visiting his family mainly at weekends – a situation which, coupled with his womanising and excessive drinking, caused the marriage to deteriorate along with his health. Throughout it all, Hammett wrote often to his family, and on the occasion of her eighteenth birthday sent this letter to his youngest daughter – his 'Loco Princess' – who shared her mother's name.*

## THE LETTER

APO 980 (i.e., The Aleutians),
Seattle, Washington

Dearest Princess -

So now you're eighteen and I'm all out of child daughters. My family is cluttered up with grown women. There's nobody who has to say, "Sir," to me anymore and there are no more noses to wipe. I feel old and caught-up-with. But there's no use sulking about it, I guess, and I might as well try to make the best of it and welcome you into the ranks of the adult. I'm sure you'll like our little club.

As you've probably found out by now, this world of grown-ups into which you have been admitted is a very, very superior world indeed, inhabited only by people of sound, mature and mellow mentality — all of which they can of course provide simply by showing the dates on their birth certificates.

But what you may not yet have noticed is that all these people stand on their own feet as independently as all get-out, being beholden to their fellows only for food, shelter, clothing, safety, happiness, love, life and picture post cards.

Another thing you'll discover is that one of the chief differences – some cynics say it's the only difference – between a child and an adult is a child is under some sort of obligation to grow, while an adult doesn't have to if he doesn't want to. Isn't he already grown up? What do you want 'im to do? Try to make himself into God or something?

You'll *love* our little club.

Actually, it's nice thinking of you as grown up, darling. You were a nice child and you'll make a fine woman and it may not be necessary to disown you for many, many years to come.

Until then, much love and kisses,

Papa

## LETTER 22
## GOOD-NIGHT, MY SACRED OLD FATHER
William James to Henry James Sr
*14 December 1882*

*In December 1882, whilst visiting Paris, William James, the 'Father of American psychology' and leading philosopher, received word that his father's ill-health had deteriorated at the family home in the US, but that William should for the moment stay in Europe and await further instruction. On returning immediately to England, he discovered that his brother, the novelist Henry James, had already left his London home for New York, where his sister was already caring for their father. Acutely aware that he may ultimately reach his father's bedside too late, William wrote him the following letter – a beautiful farewell that sadly arrived a day too late, but which was subsequently read aloud by Henry at their father's grave. William did not see his father again.*

# THE LETTER

Bolton St.

London

Dec. 14, 1882

DARLING OLD FATHER,—Two letters, one from my
Alice last night, and one from Aunt Kate to Harry
just now, have somewhat dispelled the mystery in
which the telegrams left your condition; and
although their news is several days earlier than the
telegrams, I am free to suppose that the latter
report only an aggravation of the symptoms the
letters describe. It is far more agreeable to think of
this than of some dreadful unknown and sudden
malady.

We have been so long accustomed to the
hypothesis of your being taken away from us,
especially during the past ten months, that the
thought that this may be your last illness conveys
no very sudden shock. You are old enough, you've
given your message to the world in many ways and
will not be forgotten; you are here left alone, and
on the other side, let us hope and pray, dear, dear
old Mother is waiting for you to join her. If you
go, it will not be an inharmonious thing. Only, if

you are still in possession of your normal
consciousness, I should like to see you once again
before we part. I stayed here only in obedience to
the last telegram, and am waiting now for Harry—
who knows the exact state of my mind, and who
will know yours—to telegraph again what I shall
do. Meanwhile, my blessed old Father, I scribble
this line (which may reach you though I should
come too late), just to tell you how full of the
tenderest memories and feelings about you my
heart has for the last few days been filled. In that
mysterious gulf of the past into which the present
soon will fall and go back and back, yours is still
for me the central figure. All my intellectual life I
derive from you; and though we have often seemed
at odds in the expression thereof, I'm sure there is
a harmony somewhere, and that our strivings will
combine. What my debt to you is goes beyond all
my power of estimating,—so early, so penetrating
and so constant has been the influence. You need
be in no anxiety about your literary remains. I will
see them well taken care of, and that your words
shall not suffer for being concealed. At Paris I heard
that Milsand, whose name you may remember in
the "Revue des Deux Mondes" and elsewhere, was
an admirer of the "Secret of Swedenborg," and
Hodgson told me your last book had deeply

impressed him. So will it be; especially, I think, if a collection of *extracts* from your various writings were published, after the manner of the extracts from Carlyle, Ruskin, & Co. I have long thought such a volume would be the best monument to you.—As for us; we shall live on each in his way,—feeling somewhat unprotected, old as we are, for the absence of the parental bosoms as a refuge, but holding fast together in that common sacred memory. We will stand by each other and by Alice, try to transmit the torch in our offspring as you did in us, and when the time comes for being gathered in, I pray we may, if not all, some at least, be as ripe as you. As for myself, I know what trouble I've given you at various times through my peculiarities; and as my own boys grow up, I shall learn more and more of the kind of trial you had to overcome in superintending the development of a creature different from yourself, for whom you felt responsible. I say this merely to show how my *sympathy* with you is likely to grow much livelier, rather than to fade—and not for the sake of regrets.—As for the other side, and Mother, and our all possibly meeting, I can't say anything. More than ever at this moment do I feel that if that were true, all would be solved and justified. And it comes strangely over me in bidding you good-bye how a life is but a day and expresses mainly but a single note. It is so much like the act of bidding an ordinary good-night. Good-night, my sacred old Father! If I don't see you again—Farewell! a blessed farewell!

Your
William

'WHAT MY DEBT TO
YOU IS GOES BEYOND
ALL MY POWER OF
ESTIMATING, — SO
EARLY, SO PENETRATING
AND SO CONSTANT HAS
BEEN THE INFLUENCE'

— *William James*

## LETTER 23
## I AM AWFULLY COMFORTABLE
Rudyard Kipling, John Kipling and
Colonel Lionel Charles Dunsterville
*1915*

*When World War I broke out in 1914, fiercely patriotic*
The Jungle Book *author Rudyard Kipling encouraged his*
*seventeen-year-old son, John, to fight for their country.*
*John did just that and in August of the next year, now*
*a fully-trained soldier in the Irish Guard, he made his*
*way to France where his father was already working*
*as a war correspondent. John Kipling kept in touch*
*with his parents by letter, and Rudyard Kipling wrote*
*back to his son daily, as evidenced by the following*
*exchange. Tragically, just a month after arriving in*
*France, weeks after his eighteenth birthday, John*
*Kipling was killed at the Battle of Loos. Two months*
*later, presuming the death of his son, Kipling wrote to*
*his close friend, Colonel Lionel Charles Dunsterville.*

## THE LETTERS

Somewhere in France
Friday 20th August

Dear F-

Here we are billeted in a splendid little village
nestling among the downs about 20 miles from the
firing line. It is an awfully nice place – a typical
French village about the size of Burwash Wield.

I have the great luck of being billeted with the
Mayor, who is also the school master, in his house.
I am awfully comfortable, having a feather bed with
sheets & a sitting room for 3 of us, the whole
place being absolutely spotlessly clean. The old
Mayor is a topping old fellow who can't speak a
word of English, but the kindest chap you ever met
& awfully funny. He possesses a very pretty
daughter – Marcelle – who is awfully nice and we
get on very well.

The old lady too is A1 & they will do anything
for one. The only disadvantage is that there is very
little food & what there is is very 2nd rate. All the
other Regiments have gutted the place, & one can't
get a cigarette for love or money. Our food in the
Mess is mostly bully beef & jam.

I can't of course tell you where this place is, but it is quite near the place I told you I thought we would go. The country is looking awfully nice, with all the crops to get in yet.

We haven't had any letters yet since we left, but are hoping that they will arrive tomorrow.

Motor bike despatch riders abound here, tearing along at fearsome speeds, and big lorries going "all out".

How goes old Vincent?

The French here are the dirtiest I ever saw, their ideas of hotels are simply unspeakable!! The men talking French are screamingly funny, but they manage to get on very well with the French girls.

As we have to censor all the letters at our platoon we get some very funny things; also some rather pathetic ones.

The men are sticking it wonderfully considering they haven't had a square meal since they left England. The idea is I believe that we stay here a fortnight before we go up to the trenches but one can never tell from one moment to the next what is going to happen to one next.

Please send me

a pair of my ordinary pyjamas
that stiff hair brush

Grayson has discovered a French girl who rather resembles Gaby in appearance and very much so in morals so he is quite happy.

You might send me out one of those letter block letters & envelopes all in one.

Please remember me to Jerry

Much love to yourself
John

\* \* \*

Hotel Brighton,
218, Rue de Rivoli,
Paris.
Aug. 25. 1915. 7.30 p.m.

Dear old man –

As I leave tomorrow at a perfectly ungodly hour in order that there may be time at the railway station to examine the passports, I write my little daily letter to you now. I hope to be in Folkestone by 6 o'clock tomorrow evening but this is a deceitful world and there have been several delays in the Channel boats. I expect the submarines are on the rampage again. Yesterday's train went off crowded to the lee-scuppers (if that is the right word) on account of no boat going the day before.

I have been working all day at my accounts of my travels and saying pretty things about the French Army. I really think that they are excellent and I expect as time goes on, you will be of that opinion too. Really, there isn't much difference between the way in which the officers of the English and French armies look at things. I was talking the other night "Somewhere in France" with a delightful old General. We were some miles from a town and the German and French search-lights were playing all around us. I asked him if he knew who was his opposite number on the Hun side. "Quite well," he said. "I've known him for months." (He told me his name.) "He's an old man and I think he has gout. Every now and again I keep him awake all night with my big guns. He always loses his temper. He gets excited and begins to fire away all round the landscape. I should say he cost Germany a lot in ammunition." Now isn't that very much as an English officer would talk.

11 p.m. Just back from an idiotic cinema theatre at the Ambassadeurs. There were lots of faked pictures of the war and the only funny turn was

about a kid who was spanked for throwing stones into a river where a man was fishing. So he went back to his father's caravan (he was a gipsy), got a crocodile's skin and fastened it over his dog. Well, as you can imagine the sight of a sky-blue crocodile on four legs running at him like Hell rather upset the fisherman and then the dog-crocodile got loose all over the country and the usual upsets and panics followed.

*Thursday morn 9 a.m.* Just off for Boulogne and have just received copy of your letter of 20th describing your billet with the Mayor and the maid Marcelle and the immoral luck of Grayson and local Gaby. I'm sorry about the food but Bateman's will do its best to supplement. You ought to get a whole lot of letters from me when you arrive as I've written you regularly. Now for the Gare du Nord and a hell of a crush at the station.

Ever,
Dad

\* \* \*

Saturday Sept 25th
5.30 p.m.

Dear F –

Just a hurried line as we start off tonight. The front line trenches are nine miles off from here so it wont be a very long march.

This is THE great effort to break through & end the war.

The guns have been going deafeningly all day, without a single stop.

We have to push through at all costs so we won't have much time in the trenches, which is great luck.

Funny to think one will be in the thick of it tomorrow.

One's first experience of shell fire not in the trenches but in the open.

This is one of the advantages of a Flying Division, you have to keep moving.

We marched 18 miles last night in the pouring wet.

It came down in sheets steadily.

They are staking a tremendous lot on this great advancing movement as if it succeeds the war won't go on for long.

You have no idea what enormous issues depend on the next few days.

This will be my last letter most likely for some time as we won't get any time for writing this next week, but I will try & send Field post cards.

> Well so long old dears.
> Dear love
> John.

Love to Jerry.
> JK

* * *

Bateman's / Burwash / Sussex / Nov. 12. 1915.

Dear Lionel

[...]

Our boy was reported "wounded and missing"
since Sep. 27 – the battle of Loos and we've heard
nothing official since that date. But all we can pick
up from the men points to the fact that he is dead
and probably wiped out by shell fire.

However, he had his heart's desire and he didn't
have a long time in trenches. The Guards advanced
on a front of two platoons for each battalion. He
led the right platoon over a mile of open ground
in the face of shell and machine-gun fire and was
dropped at the further limit of the advance, after
having emptied his pistol into a house full of
German machine guns. His Commanding Officer
and his company commander told me how he he
led 'em: and the wounded have confirmed it. He
was senior ensign tho' only 18 years and 6 weeks,
had worked like the devil for a year at Warley and
knew his Irish to the ground. He was reported on
as one of the best subalterns and was gym
instructor and signaller. It was a short life. I'm
sorry that all the year's work ended in that one

afternoon but - lots of people are in our position and it's something to have bred a man. The wife is standing it wonderfully tho' she of course clings to the bare hope of his being a prisoner. I've seen what shells can do and I don't.

We're pounding on in our perfectly insane English fashion. The boys at the front are cheery enough, (we've got rather a lot of artillery) and the Hun is being killed daily. It's the old story. All the victories were on Napoleon's side all through and yet he didn't somehow get further than St. Helena.

[...]

Now, my dear old man, try and look after yourself a bit and keep fit. We've a hell of a year ahead of us but after that I think we'll be through.

Ever,

      Rudyard

## LETTER 24
## I'LL ALWAYS BE YOUR LITTLE GIRL
Lily Collins to Phil Collins
*2017*

*Lily Collins was born in 1989 in south-west England to Jill Tavelman and Phil Collins. At the age of six, her parents divorced and her father moved far away, leading to a twenty-year long-distance relationship with a globally famous father who regularly travelled the world performing to adoring crowds of fans. She has since become a star in her own right as an acclaimed actor, and in 2017 wrote* Unfiltered: No Shame, No Regrets, Just Me *in which, amongst a collection of personal essays about the struggles faced by young women of today, can be found this letter to her father.*

## THE LETTER

Dear Dad,

No matter how old I get, I'll always be your little
girl. No matter how mature I am (or like to think
I am), I'll always value your opinion. I'll always
need you. I'll always want you to check in with
me no matter how much you think it will annoy
me. Even if it does annoy me, I'll secretly love it.
When I call you out on something that has upset
or annoyed me, please don't mistake my criticism
for loving you any less. Don't think that you've
done something that can't be fixed. It's not about
fixing; it's about moving forward knowing that
things can change. I'm not counting up your past
mistakes and keeping score and using them against
you. I'm calling attention to the way certain
actions make me feel and how they can be avoided
going forward. It's important for us both to
acknowledge not only the good things that make
us happy, but also the unfortunate ones that hurt
us. I want to celebrate my successes and share my
failures with you, no matter how big or small. I
know I'm technically an adult now but I still need
your help. Want your help. And despite my best
efforts to convince myself I don't need your
approval, I still find myself seeking to be noticed,

desperate for your hugs, craving your attention and affirmations. I still have those little-girl fears of saying something that might frustrate you. And I never want to let you down. But there will be times that I mess up. We all do it. Even you do it. But know that, even in all those "mess-ups," my intention was always to make you proud. I know you've told me that I do and that you love me. Still, it's nice to be reminded, especially when we're far apart. A quick call or even a short text or email to say hi every once in a while will do the job. Check in with me. You may think I'm busy, and I am busy, but even if I can't look at my phone for hours, at the end of the day I'd love to see that you were thinking of me. Because I'm definitely thinking of you.

Sometimes I try to be the bigger person, to take the high road, but you are the parent here. There are some things that I expect you to do—hope you would want to do—no matter how old I get. To be there to talk to, to learn from. To be someone who doesn't just show up for the fun stuff but is also there for the rough and tough and extremely-hard-to-deal-with stuff. We all make choices and, although I don't excuse some of yours, at the end of the day we can't rewrite the past. I'm learning how to accept your actions and vocalize how they made me feel. I accept and honor the sadness and anger I felt toward the things you did or didn't do, did or didn't give me. I've learned a lot and my eyes and heart are wide open. I now understand that my frustrations surrounding our communication are not about changing you but accepting you as you are.

I, however, am changing. I'm getting to know who I am, peeling back all the layers, and figuring out who I am underneath everything. Finding my way out of dark times and deciphering what makes me me. I'd like for you to meet who I'm finding. I'd love for you to take the time to get to know her and be part of that process. Because, I have to say, she's pretty damn special. I forgive you for not always being there when I needed and for not being the dad I expected. I forgive the mistakes you made. And although it may seem like it's too late, it's not. There's still so much time to move forward. And I want to. I'm inviting you to join me. I love you with all of my heart, more than you'll ever know, and am so thankful for you.

I'll always be your little girl.

Love Always and Forever,

Me x

## LETTER 25
## YOUR EDUCATION
Mohandas Gandhi to his son
*25 March 1909*

*Before he became a leader of the nationalist movement*
*against British rule in India, Mohandas Gandhi fought*
*for the rights of Indians in South Africa. For this, he*
*was imprisoned in Pretoria on four different occasions.*
*This letter was written to his second son, Manilal,*
*sixteen, during his third incarceration. In 1915 Gandhi*
*returned to India to work for independence from*
*Britain and reformation of the caste system. Following*
*the painful partition of India and Pakistan in 1947,*
*Mohandas was assassinated by a Hindu fanatic*
*enraged by his tolerance of Muslims. Manilal followed*
*in his father's footsteps and, like him, was imprisoned*
*in both India and South Africa for his actions on behalf*
*of humans rights and social justice.*

## THE LETTER

My dear Son,

I have a right to write one letter per month and
receive also one letter per month. It became a quest
as to whom I should write. I thought of Mr. Ritch,
Mr. Polak and you. I chose you as you have been
nearest my thoughts in all my reading. As for
myself I must not, I am not allowed to say much. I
am quite at peace and none need worry about me.

I hope mother [Kasturba Gandhi] is now quite
well. I know several letters from you have been
received but they have not been given to me. The
Deputy Governor was good enough to tell me that
she was getting on well. Does she now walk about
freely? I hope she and all of you would continue to
take sago and milk in the morning. And now about
yourself. How are you? Although I think you are
well able to bear all the burden I have placed on
your shoulders and that you are doing it quite
cheerfully, I have often felt that you require greater
personal guidance than I have been able to give
you. I know too that you have sometimes felt that
your education was being neglected. Now I have

read a great deal in the prison. I have been reading Emerson, Ruskin, Mazzini. I have also been reading the *Upanishads*. All confirm the view that education does not mean knowledge of letters but it means character building. It means a knowledge of duty. Our own word [केळवणी] literally means training. If this be the true view, and it is to my mind the only true view, you are receiving the best education – training – possible. What can be better than that you should have the opportunity of nursing mother and cheerfully bearing her ill-temper, or than looking after Chanchi [wife of Harilal Gandhi] and anticipating her wants, and behaving to her so as not to make her feel the want of Harilal [then in gaol as a passive resister] or again than being guardian to Ramdas and Devadas? If you succeed in doing this well, you have received more than half your education. I was much struck by Nathuramji's introduction to the *Upanishad*. He says that the Brahmacharya stage i.e. the first stage is like the last that is the *sanyasin* stage. This is true. Amusement only continues during the age of innocence that is up to 12 years only. As soon as a boy reaches the age of discretion he is taught to realize his responsibility. Every boy from such age onward should practise continence in thought and deed, truth and the not taking of any life. This to him must not be an irksome learning and practice but it should be his enjoyment. I can recall to my mind several such boys in Rajkot. Let me tell you that when I was younger than you are, my keenest enjoyment was to nurse my father. Of amusement, after I was 12 I had little or none. If you practise the three virtues, if they become part of your life, so far as I am concerned, you will have completed your education – your training. Armed with them, believe me, you will earn your bread in any part of the world, and you will have paved the way to acquire a true knowledge of the soul, yourself and God. This does not mean that you should not receive instructions in letters. That you should and you are doing. But it is a thing over which you should not fret yourself. You have plenty of time for it, and after all you are to receive such instruction in order that your training may be of use to the others.

Remember please that henceforth our lot is poverty. The more I think of it, the more I feel that is is more blessed to be poor than to be rich. The uses of poverty are sweeter than those of riches.

You have taken the sacred thread. I want you to live up to it. It appears that leaving one's bed before sunrise is almost indispensable for proper worship. Do therefore try to keep regular hours. I have thought much over it and read something also. I respectfully disagree with the Swamiji in his propaganda. I think that the adoption of the sacred thread by those who have for ages given it up is a mistake. As it is we have too much of the false division between *shudras* and others. The sacred thread is therefore today rather a hindrance than a help. I should like to elaborate this view but I cannot for the present. I am aware that I am expressing these views before one who has made a life-long study of the subject. Yet I thought that I would pass on to the Swamiji what I have been thinking over. I have studied the *Gayatri*. I like the words. I have also studied the book the Swamiji gave me. I have derived much benefit from its perusal. It makes me more inquisitive about the life of Swami Dayanand. [His interpretation of] the *Gayatri* and several *mantras* of the *Vajasaneya Upanishad* is totally different from that given by the orthodox school. Now which meaning is correct? I do not know. I hesitate straightaway to accept the revolutionary method of interpretations suggest by Swami Dayanand. I would much like to learn through the Swamiji's lips. I hope he will not leave before I am out, but if he does leave, he will kindly leave all the literature he can or can send it from India. I should also like to know what the orthodox school has said about Swami Dayanand's teaching. Please thank the Swamiji for the handmade socks and gloves he has sent me. And get his address in India. Show the whole of this letter to the Swamiji and let me know what he says.

Do give ample work to the gardening, actual digging, hoeing etc. We have to live upon it in future. And you should be the expert gardener of the family. Keep your tools in their respective places and keep them absolutely clean. In your lessons you should give a great deal of attention to mathematics and Sanskrit. The latter is absolutely necessary for you. Both these studies are difficult in after life. You will not neglect your music. You should make a selection of all good passages, hymns and verses, whether in English, Gujarati or Hindi, and write them out in your best hand in a book. The collection at the end of the year will be most valuable. All these things you can do easily if you are methodical. Never get agitated and think you have too much to do and then worry over what to do first. This you will find in practice if you are patient and take care of your virtues. I hope you are keeping an accurate account. It should be kept of every penny spent for the household.

Please tell Maganlal that I would advise him to

read Emerson's essays. Those essays are worth studying. He should read them and mark the important passages and finally copy them out in a note book. The essays to my mind contain the teaching of Indian wisdom in a Western guide. It is refreshing to see our own sometimes differently fashioned. He should also try to read Tolstoy's *Kingdom of God is Within You*. The English of the translation is very simple. What is more Tolstoy practises what he teaches.

I hope the evening service continues and that you attend the Sunday service at the Wests.

As soon as you have read and understood my letter you may commence writing your reply. Let it be as long as you want to make it.

And now I close with love to all from father.

## LETTER 26
## I OFTEN WONDER HOW
## YOU FEEL ABOUT ME
Spalding Gray to his father
*22 September 1977*

*In September of 1977, shortly after the ten-year
anniversary of his mother's death, famed writer and
monologuist Spalding Gray borrowed a car and set off
on a 3000-mile trip from California to New York.
He reached Las Vegas in twelve hours, checked into a
motel and found a bar, and when the sun rose the
next morning found himself spending the first of six
days in jail charged with 'vagrancy'. A few days into
his stay, having spent countless hours reflecting on his
life and current predicament, he wrote a letter to
his father. Years later, it was discovered in one of
his journals; it is unknown whether his father
ever received a copy.*

# THE LETTER

Sept. 22, 1977

Dear Dad,

I've seen a lot of crazy things but this one takes the
cake. I am a prisoner in Clark County Jail in Las
Vegas. I mean, I would never have dreamed such a
thing could come to pass. Someone in Santa Cruz
loaned me a car to drive to New York, so I started
by driving twelve hours straight to Las Vegas. I got
in about 9:30 pm, Monday night, took a motel,
washed up, and went out for a walk on the strip. I
was dressed well with white pants and clean shirt.
Two cops, in two different cars, stopped me. I did
not have my ID with (a mistake I know) me, so
they handcuffed me and ran me in. I spent the
night in a detention "cooler" standing with about
24 men, all of us in prison outfits. They stripped
me and sprayed with DDT, put me in a prison
outfit, and photographed and fingerprinted me. All
of this was like some mad dream. I mean I was
stone sober. I had not broken any law I knew of,
but I went along with it all ... just played it cool.
About five in the morning, they took us down in
the basement for breakfast and then I was locked

up in a cell with forty prisoners, some in for armed robbery, some in for rape, murder, trespassing, you name it.

Well, I just work at staying calm for the first two days. I mainly stayed in my bed and watched what was going on. It was all like a movie, but a little too real. On my second day here, someone stabbed himself with a wire and was taken away.

I find the only way for me to stay sane is to talk with the prisoners about their lives and that has helped, but what stories. I mean it's all like out of a movie. The worst thing that is going on is that the jail guards will not let me make a call to Liz to get bail money, and Vegas is such a rip-off town I don't know when my hearing will be. My bail is set at $250.00 which is not bad. I don't know what's happened to my car or any of my bags and money. They were all left at the motel and I don't trust them there either. Santa Cruz was paradise ... full of love and Vegas is hell ... full of hate and money mad zombies. It's a long story. I've tried everything to get out of here and feel like a helpless child.

So ... I've had some time to do some real thinking. I've sort of gone over my life ... kind of figuring out how or why I was here ... how I got into this jam. One of the things I've come up with in thinking about my past—nothing to do with why I'm here—but having to do with our relationship, is that I've felt we have never been very close to one another. I mean, we've had some times in the past. I remember you helping me with algebra, and going frost fishing together, and you doing the stop watch while I ran around the block. These events are all part of a long gone past and I wonder what's happening now. I get so little time in Rhode Island, so we hardly have a chance to talk. I mean, it's not that I think you don't love me. Your helping me with the psychiatrist last winter made me feel that you still cared for me and wanted to help. Perhaps it's been a little one sided and I have not showed you that I care, but I want to take time now to thank you for that help last winter and I do remember a good visit with you at Christmas. I think I'm feeling age coming on me (you know all about that) and I want to have contact with you while there is some time left … not trying to be morbid but just realistic.

I guess I have some heavy questions. I don't want to get heavy like Rocky, but I often wonder how you feel about me and I don't mean just being nice … I'm not sure what I mean. I just feel strange about our relationship. I think that I did a lot of shutting down after mom's death, when we were together at Shady Hill, and that might have been a time together. Although, the visit in New York was good but I do feel bad about one past event. Shortly after mom's death, I was in the Robert Lowell play in N.Y.C., and you called to say you'd like to come down and I did not encourage you to do it because I was embarrassed that it was such a small role. After all was said and done, I was sorry I did not ask you down. Anyway, that's water under the bridge. I think it was a problem of false pride.

I am going through a lot of good and bad turmoil in my life now. I think it's change, and growing up, and part of it all, but I need to know where we are at. I don't feel we make contact, and that we are both uptight around each other. I'm sure a lot of it comes from not seeing each other much, but I can never tell if you want me at your home or if you are just being polite ... doing what you think a father should do. I know you say you want me there but I'm missing the feeling. I think feeling is very important to me now and I want to feel where I'm at when I'm at it. I mean, I want to feel a little more. I've done all the thinking I want to do for a while. I've been so serious all these years and I had a good chance to loosen up in California (not in Vegas).

Anyway, why don't you write me a letter? I hardly ever hear from you by mail and would enjoy a letter. If all goes well, I hope to be back in N.Y.C. on October third. I don't want to go to Europe. I want to do a new work. There is a meeting in N.Y.C. about our European tour. It's tonight and I was going to call in my vote, but my jailer won't even lend me an ear. They just grin and say "Sure thing," "We'll see what we can do," etc. But I would like to hear from you. Nothing heavy, just some response. I feel I missed you somewhere along the line. Why do you think that is?

I worry about Gram and I wonder how she is. I want to come home for Christmas and hope to take three or four days off. Please send my love to Sis [Alice Gray, whom his father married two years after the death of Gray's mother], Gram, Chan, and Bianca. I don't have C&B's address, or I would have written them. I hope to be out of here soon and off to the Grand Canyon (if I still have a car).

Much love,
Spud

## LETTER 27
## FATHER, DON'T TURN AWAY FROM ME
Katherine Mansfield to her father
*30 October 1921*

*Katherine Mansfield, born Kathleen Mansfield*
*Beauchamp, left her childhood home in Wellington, New*
*Zealand, at the age of twenty, never to return. In*
*contrast with her siblings, she led a tumultuous personal*
*life, reeling with erratic and socially unacceptable*
*behaviour that strained her relationship with her staid,*
*upright parents. Nevertheless, her father, Harold,*
*continued to provide her with an annual allowance*
*throughout her life. Katherine was diagnosed with active*
*tuberculosis in 1917, and the following year was found to*
*have a long-simmering gonococcal infection that had*
*affected her heart. She refused to enter a sanatorium*
*and underwent questionable treatments that may have*
*hastened her decline. Her health was rapidly failing*
*when she penned this poignant, yearning letter to her*
*father, and she suffered a fatal pulmonary haemorrhage*
*just over a year later.*

# THE LETTER

If Chaddie or Jeanne had developed consumption husbands or no husbands they would surely have appealed to you. One does turn to ones father however old one is. Had I forfeited the right to do so? Perhaps . . . There is no reason, Father dear, that you should go on loving me through thick and thin. I see that. And I have been an extraordinarily unsatisfactory and disappointing child.

But in spite of everything, one gets shot in the wing and one believes that 'home' will receive one and cherish one. When we were together in France I was happy with you as I had always longed to be but when I knew that you grudged me the money it was simply torture. I did not know what to say about it. I waited until I saw if I could earn more myself at that time. But it was not possible. Then I had waited so long that it seemed impossible to write. Then I was so seriously ill that I was not in a state to write to anybody. And by the time that crisis was over it seemed to me my sin of silence was too great to beg forgiveness, and so it has gone on.

But I cannot bear it any longer. I must come to you and at least acknowledge my fault. I must at least tell you, even though the time has passed when you wish to listen, that never for a moment, in my folly and my fear, have I ceased to love you and to honour you. I have punished myself so cruelly that I couldn't suffer more.

Father don't turn away from me, darling. If you cannot take me back into your heart believe me when I say I am

Your devoted deeply sorrowing child
Kass

## LETTER 28
## MY CHILDREN IS MY OWN
Spotswood Rice to his children and Katherine Diggs
*3 September 1864*

*In February 1864, an enslaved man from Glasgow,
Missouri, named Spotswood Rice escaped his job as
manager of his owner's tobacco farm and instead
enrolled with the 67th US Colored Infantry in St Louis.
Several months later, as he recovered from a bout of
chronic rheumatism in Benton Barracks military
hospital, Rice wrote two letters – the first to his
still-enslaved daughters, Mary and Corra, and the
second to their owner, Katherine Diggs – and in both
made clear his intention to rescue his children from
slavery with the help of hundreds of fellow soldiers.
His daughters never read the letter, as both were
intercepted by Diggs's brother, who happened to be the
local postmaster. Instead, they were forwarded to US
Army command in Missouri. Spotswood Rice was
reunited with his family the next year, although it's
unknown whether a showdown with Diggs occurred.*

## THE LETTERS

[Benton Barracks Hospital, St. Louis, Mo.
September 3, 1864]

My Children    I take my pen in hand to rite you
A few lines to let you know that I have not forgot
you and that I want to see you as bad as ever
now my Dear Children I want you to be
contented with whatever may be your lots    be
assured that I will have you if it cost me my life
on the 28th of the mounth. 8 hundred White and
8 hundred blacke solders expects to start up the
rivore to Glasgow and above there thats to be
jeneraled by a jeneral that will give me both of
you    when they Come I expect to be with, them
and expect to get you both in return. Dont be
uneasy my children    I expect to have you. If
Diggs dont give you up this Government will and
I feel confident that I will get you    Your Miss
Kaitty said that I tried to steal you    But I'll let
her know that god never intended for man to steal
his own flesh and blood. If I had no cofidence in
God I could have confidence in her    But as it is
If I ever had any Confidence in her I have none
now and never expect to have    And I want her to

139

remember if she meets me with ten thousand soldiers she [will?] meet her enemy   I once [thought] that I had some respect for them but now my respects is worn out and have no sympathy for Slaveholders. And as for her cristianantty I expect the Devil has Such in hell You tell her from me that She is the frist Christian that I ever hard say that aman could Steal his own child especially out of human bondage

You can tell her that She can hold to you as long as she can   I never would expect to ask her again to let you come to me because I know that the devil has got her hot set againsts that that is write   now my Dear children I am a going to close my letter to you   Give my love to all enquiring friends   tell them all that we are well and want to see them very much and Corra and Mary receive the greater part of it you sefves and dont think hard of us not sending you any thing I you father have a plenty for you when I see you   Spott & Noah sends their love to both of you   Oh! My Dear children how I do want to see you

Spotswood Rice

\* \* \*

I received a leteter from Cariline telling me that you
say I tried to steal to plunder my child away from
you    now I want you to understand that mary is
my Child and she is a God given rite of my own
and you may hold on to hear as long as you can
but I want you to remembor this one thing that the
longor you keep my Child from me the longor you
will have to burn in hell and the qwicer youll get
their    for we are now makeing up a bout one
thoughsand blacke troops to Come up tharough and
wont to come through Glasgow and when we come
wo be to Copperhood rabbels and to the
Slaveholding rebbels for we dont expect to leave
them there root neor branch    but we thinke how
ever that we that have Children in the hands of you
devels we will trie your [vertues?] the day that we
enter Glasgow    I want you to understand kittey
diggs that where ever you and I meets we are
enmays to each orthere    I offered once to pay you
forty dollers for my own Child but I am glad now
that you did not accept it    Just hold on now as
long as you can and the worse it will be for you
you never in you life befor I came down hear did
you give Children any thing not eny thing whatever

141

not even a dollers worth of expencs   now you call
my children your pro[per]ty   not so with me   my
Children is my own and I expect to get them and
when I get ready to come after mary I will have
bout a powrer and autherity to bring hear away and
to exacute vengencens on them that holds my Child
you will then know how to talke to me   I will
assure that and you will know how to talk rite too
I want you now to just hold on to hear if you want
to   iff your conchosence tells thats the road go that
road and what it will brig you to kittey diggs   I
have no fears about geting mary out of your hands
this whole Government gives chear to me and you
cannot help your self

Spotswood Rice

'THE LONGOR YOU
KEEP MY CHILD FROM
ME THE LONGOR YOU
WILL HAVE TO BURN
IN HELL . . .'

— Spottswood Rice

## LETTER 29
## IT IS COLD AND DAMP HERE
Roger Mortimer to Charlie Mortimer
*1978*

*Roger Mortimer was born to a wealthy family in Chelsea, London, in 1909, and after being educated at Eton and Sandhurst fought at Dunkirk. It was in Belgium at the end of 1939 that he was knocked unconscious by a shell explosion; when he awoke, surrounded by German soldiers, he began a five-year stretch as a prisoner of war. Some years after his release, he became the racing correspondent for the* Sunday Times, *a post he held for three decades to much acclaim. He spent twenty-five years writing countless letters to his only son, Charlie. In 2012 many of those amusing, touching, exasperated, gossip-filled missives were collected to form the book* Dear Lupin, *of which this is just one, written in 1978, when Charlie was working away from home.*

# THE LETTER

Dear Lupin,

I trust your stomach is more or less under control
and that you are deriving a modicum of benefit
from those expensive pills. It is cold and damp
here and both boilers have been behaving in a
typically erratic manner. I did some baby-watching
for the Bomers last night (the baby is eleven years
old) and your mother departed for a beano at
Inkpen. I think gin was in fairly abundant supply
there and it had the customary effect of making
your mother behave like Queen Boadicea on her
return home. There are now three deaf people in
the house – Moppet, Pongo and myself. It is
sometimes fortunate that I am unable to catch
everything said to me. Your mother is still
convinced that a poltergeist whipped away a
sausage she was cooking and I expect she will call
in the Rev. Jardine for consultation. A lot of
policeman descended on Mr Luckes's house
yesterday but I have been unable to find out why. I

thought I had the cottage sold yesterday but your mother interfered at the last moment and now I am somewhat doubtful. Your Aunt Barbara is going to Jerusalem for Christmas; that ought to precipitate a new war in the Middle East. Aunt Joan goes into hospital tomorrow. I imagine David Willett is having an exciting time in Persia: my godson Richard Rome, married to a Persian, is there too. Newbury is full of people from the council estates in Thatcham doing their Christmas shopping. It would hardly be true to say that they add to the charm of the town. The tall woman with bandaged legs in the chemists in the Mall is going into semi-retirement: a sad loss, as she is easily the most reliable medical advisor in this area, particularly sound on skin blemishes and diarrhoea. A man was killed on the road at Beacon Hill on Friday: road conditions were disagreeable at the time. Mrs Cameron stayed on Thursday night: she and your mother talked incessantly; neither listened to a word the other said which was sensible as neither was saying anything really worth listening to. I had a long letter from your Great-Aunt Phyllis but could not read a word of it bar my own name and her signature.

Your affec. father,

RM

P.S. A long article on Dr Philips in the 'Newbury News'. A man from Gowrings has bought Brig. Lewis's house. The bearded man in the Newbury bookshop claims to have flogged 150 copies of my book which would be good news if I happened to believe it. Which I don't. The rather lanky young woman who worked in Jacksons in the afternoon has disappeared. I have kept a first copy of The Times for you. It might one day be valuable. 'Colonel Mad' has vanished from Lambourn: some say to gaol, others to a loony bin. Nick Gaselee won a nice race last week. There was a large photograph of him in the Sporting Life.

Mr and Mrs Cottrill are off to India for two months. Mrs Randall is giving her relatives potatoes for Christmas. I have given up smoking.

## LETTER 30
## NO DREAM CAN DO JUSTICE TO YOU
Fergal Keane to Daniel Patrick Keane
*4 February 1996*

*Fergal Keane was born in 1961 in London, but spent
much of his childhood in Ireland. He began his career
in journalism straight out of school at the age of
eighteen and within a decade he was a correspondent
for the BBC – first in Northern Ireland, and then in
South Africa and Asia – winning numerous awards for
his war dispatches, as well as his books and other
works. On 4 February 1996, three years after the death
of his own father, Keane penned this emotional letter
to a fresh arrival: his newborn son, Daniel. It was read
out on the BBC Radio 4 programme* From Our Own
Correspondent *and was an immediate hit with the
listening audience, garnering record levels of feedback
and going on to earn Keane two additional awards.*

## THE LETTER

My dear son

It is six o'clock in the morning on the island of
Hong Kong. You are asleep, cradled in my left arm,
and I am learning the art of one-handed typing.
Your mother, more tired, yet more happy than I've
ever known her, is sound asleep in the room next
door. And there is soft quiet in our apartment.
Since you've arrived, days have melted into night
and back again, and we are learning a new
grammar. A long sentence whose punctuation
marks are feeding and winding and nappy
changing, and these occasional moments of quiet.

When you're older we'll tell you that you were
born in Britain's last Asian colony in the lunar year
of the pig and that when we brought you home,
the staff of our apartment block gathered to wish
you well. 'It's a boy, so lucky, so lucky. We Chinese
love boys,' they told us. One man said you were
the first baby to be born on the block in the year
of the pig. This, he told us, was good feng shui, in
other words a positive sign for the building and
everyone who lived there. Naturally your mother

and I were only too happy to believe that. We had wanted you and waited for you, imagined you and dreamed about you, and now that you are here, no dream can do justice to you.

Outside the window now, below us on the harbour, the ferries are ploughing back and forth to Kowloon, millions are already up and moving about, and the sun is slanting through the tower blocks and out onto the flat silver waters of the South China Sea. I can see the con trail of a jet over Lamma Island and somewhere out there the last stars flickering towards the other side of the world.

We have called you Daniel Patrick, but I have been told by my Chinese friends that you should have a Chinese name as well, and this glorious dawn sky makes me think that we'll call you Son of the Eastern Star. So that later when you and I are far from Asia, perhaps standing on a beach somewhere, I can tell you of the Orient and the times and the people we knew there in the last years of the twentieth century. Your coming has turned me upside down and inside out. So much that seemed essential to me has, in the past few days, taken on a different colour. Like many foreign correspondents I know I have lived a life that on occasion has veered close to the edge: war zones, natural disasters, darkness in all its shapes and forms.

In a world of insecurity and ambition and ego it's easy to be drawn in, to take chances with our lives, to believe that what we do and what people say about it is reason enough to gamble with death. Now, looking at your sleeping face, inches away from me, listening to your occasional sigh and gurgle, I wonder how I could have ever thought glory and prizes and praise were sweeter than life.

And it's also true that I am pained, perhaps haunted is a better word, by the memory, suddenly so vivid now, of each suffering child I have come across on my journeys. To tell you the truth, it's nearly too much to bear at this moment to even think of children being hurt and abused and killed. And yet, looking at you, the images come flooding back.

Ten-year-old Ani Mikail dying from napalm burns on a hillside in Eritrea, how his voice cried out, growing ever more faint when the wind blew dust onto his wounds.

The two brothers, Domingo and Juste in Menongue, southern Angola. Juste, three years old and blind, dying from malnutrition, being carried on 10-year-old Domingo's back. And Domingo's words to me: "He was nice before, but now he has the hunger."

Last October in Afghanistan, while you were growing inside your mother, I met Charja, age 12, motherless, fatherless, guiding me through the grey ruins of her home. Everything was gone, she told me. And I knew that for all her tender years she had learned more about loss that I would likely understand in a lifetime.

There is one last memory, of Rwanda, and the churchyard of the parish of Nyarabuye, where, in a ransacked classroom, I found a mother and her three young children huddled together where they had been beaten to death. The children had died holding onto their mother, that instinct we all learn from birth and in one way or another cling to until we die.

Daniel, these memories explain some of the fierce protectiveness I feel for you, the tenderness and the occasional moments of blind terror when I imagine anything happening to you. But there is something more, a story from long ago that I will tell you face to face, father to son, when you are older. It's a very personal story but it is part of the picture. It has to do with the long lines of blood and family, about our lives and how we can get lost in them, and if we're lucky find our way of again into the sunlight.

It begins 35 years ago in a big city on a January morning with snow on the ground and a woman walking to hospital to have her first baby. She is in her early twenties and the city is still strange to her, bigger and noisier than the easy streets and gentle hills of her distant home. She's walking because there is no money and everything of value has been pawned to pay for the alcohol to which her husband has become addicted.

On the way a taxi driver notices her sitting exhausted and cold in the doorway of a shop and he takes her to hospital for free. Later that day she gives birth to a baby boy and, just as you are to me, he is the best thing she has ever seen. Her husband comes that night and weeps with joy when he sees his son. He is truly happy. Hungover, broke, but in his own way happy, for they were both young and in love with each other, and their son.

But, Daniel, time had some bad surprises in store for them. The cancer of alcoholism ate away at the man and he lost his family. This was not something he meant to do or wanted to do, it just was. When you are older, my son, you will learn about how complicated life becomes. How we can lose our way and people get hurt inside and out. By the time his son had grown up, the man lived

away from his family, on his own in a
one-roomed flat, living and dying for the bottle.
He died on the 5th of January, one day before the
anniversary of his son's birth all those years before
in that snowbound city. But his son was too far
away to hear his last words, his final breath, and
all the things they might have wished to say to
one another were left unspoken.

Yet, now Daniel, when you let out your first
powerful cry in the delivery room and I became a
father, I thought of your grandfather, and, foolish
though it may seem, hoped that in some way he
could hear, across the infinity between the living
and the dead, your proud statement of arrival.
For if he could hear, he would recognise the
distinct voice of family, the sound of hope, of
new beginnings that you and all your innocence
and freshness have brought to the world.

'NOW THAT YOU ARE
HERE, NO DREAM CAN
DO JUSTICE TO YOU'

— Fergal Keane

## PERMISSION CREDITS

Every effort has been made to trace copyright holders and obtain their permission for the use of copyright material. The publisher apologises for any errors or omissions and would be grateful if notified of any corrections that should be incorporated in future reprints or editions of this book.

**LETTER 1** © 2020 Estate of Samuel Bernstein. Used by permission of The Leonard Bernstein Office, Inc. Letter obtained from the Serge Koussevitzky Collection, Music Division, Library of Congress.

**LETTER 4** Reprinted with the kind permission of Jonathan Bailey & Triton Klugh.

**LETTER 5** From *Letters of Ted Hughes* by Ted Hughes, published by Faber and Faber. / Letter "To Nicholas Hughes [Undated 1986]" from *Letters of Ted Hughes* selected and edited by Christopher Reid. Letters © 2007 by The Estate of Ted Hughes. Reprinted by permission of Farrar, Straus and Giroux.

**LETTER 6** Excerpt(s) from *Saul Bellow: Letters* by Saul Bellow, edited by Benjamin Taylor, copyright © 2010 by Janis Bellow. Used by permission of Viking Books, an imprint of Penguin Publishing Group, a division of Penguin Random House LLC. All rights reserved. / Copyright © 2010, The Estate of Saul Bellow, used by permission of The Wylie Agency (UK) Limited.

**LETTER 8** Excerpt from *The Diary of a Young Girl: The Definitive Edition* by Anne Frank, edited by Otto H. Frank and Mirjam Pressler, translated by Susan Massotty, translation copyright © 1995 by Penguin Random House LLC. Used by permission of Doubleday, an imprint of the Knopf Doubleday Publishing Group, a division of Penguin Random House LLC. All rights reserved. / 471 words from *The Diary of a Young Girl* by Anne Frank translated by Mirjam Pressler and Susan Massotty (Viking 1997) (Puffin Books 1997) (Doubleday 2001) (Puffin Books 2002, 2019) Copyright © The Anne Frank – Fonds, Basle, Switzerland, 1991, 2002. English translation copyright © Doubleday, a division of Random House, Inc., 1995, 2002.

**LETTER 9** Reprinted by kind permission of Rick and Nicholas Reed.

**LETTER 12** Reprinted by permission of Frank Ferrante Productions, Inc.

**LETTER 18** From *Kurt Vonnegut: Letters* by Kurt Vonnegut, edited by Dan Wakefield, Published by Vintage Classics, Reprinted by

## ACKNOWLEDGEMENTS

It requires a dedicated team of incredibly patient people to bring the Letters of Note books to life, and this page serves as a heartfelt thank you to every single one of them, beginning with my wife, Karina – not just for her emotional support during such stressful times, but for the vital role she has played as Permissions Editor on many of the books in this series. Special mention, also, to my excellent editor at Canongate Books, Hannah Knowles, who has somehow managed to stay focused despite the problems I have continued to throw her way.

Equally sincere thanks to all of the following: Teddy Angert and Jake Liebers, whose research skills have helped make these volumes as strong as they are; Rachel Thorne and Sasmita Sinha for their crucial work on the permissions front; the one and only Jamie Byng, whose vision and enthusiasm for this series has proven invaluable; all at Canongate Books, including but not limited to Rafi Romaya, Kate Gibb, Vicki Rutherford and Leila Cruickshank; my dear family at Letters Live: Jamie, Adam Ackland, Benedict Cumberbatch, Aimie Sullivan, Amelia Richards, and Nick Allott; my agent, Caroline Michel, and everyone else at Peters, Fraser & Dunlop; the many illustrators who have worked on the beautiful covers in this series; the talented performers who have lent their stunning voices not just to Letters Live, but also to the Letters of Note audiobooks; Patti Pirooz; every single archivist and librarian in the world; everyone at Unbound; the team at the Wylie Agency for their assistance and understanding; my foreign publishers for their continued support; and, crucially, my family, for putting up with me during this process.

Finally, and most importantly, thank you to all of the letter writers whose words feature in these books.

## ALSO AVAILABLE

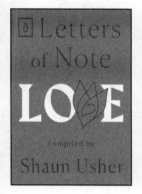 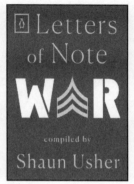 

**LETTERS OF NOTE: LOVE**

**LETTERS OF NOTE: WAR**

**LETTERS OF NOTE: MUSIC**

**LETTERS OF NOTE: CATS**

**LETTERS OF NOTE
VOLUMES 1-4 BOXED SET**

**LETTERS OF NOTE: ART**

**LETTERS OF NOTE: MOTHERS**

**LETTERS OF NOTE: FATHERS**

**LETTERS OF NOTE: OUTER SPACE**

**LETTERS OF NOTE: SEX**

**LETTERS OF NOTE: NEW YORK CITY**

**LETTERS OF NOTE: DOGS**

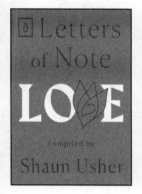 PENGUIN BOOKS

Ready to find your next great read? Let us help. Visit prh.com/nextread